D0938823

A MAN'S WOMAN

A MAN'S WOMAN

By FRANK NORRIS

AMS PRESS

NEW YORK

Reprinted from the edition of 1900, New York
First AMS EDITION published 1970
Manufactured in the United States of America

Library of Congress Catalogue Card Number: 71-108125
SBN: 404-04789-0

AMS PRESS, INC.
NEW YORK, N. Y. 10003

Dedicated to

DR. ALBERT J. HOUSTON

A MAN'S WOMAN

I.

At four o'clock in the morning everybody in the tent was still asleep, exhausted by the terrible march of the previous day. The hummocky ice and pressure-ridges that Bennett had foreseen had at last been met with, and, though camp had been broken at six o'clock and though men and dogs had hauled and tugged and wrestled with the heavy sledges until five o'clock in the afternoon, only a mile and a half had been covered. But though the progress was slow, it was yet progress. It was not the harrowing, heart-breaking immobility of those long months aboard the Freja. Every yard to the southward, though won at the expense of a battle with the ice, brought them nearer to Wrangel Island and ultimate safety.

Then, too, at supper-time the unexpected had happened. Bennett, moved no doubt by their weakened condition, had dealt out extra rations to each man: one and two-thirds ounces of butter and six and two-thirds ounces of aleuronate bread—a veritable luxury after the unvarying diet of pemmican, lime juice, and dried potatoes of the past fortnight. The men had got into their sleeping-bags early, and until four o'clock in the morning had slept profoundly, inert, stupefied, almost without movement. But a few minutes after four o'clock Bennett awoke. He was usually up about half an hour before the others. On the day before he had been able to get a meridian altitude of the sun, and was anxious to complete his calculations as to the expedition's position on the chart that he had begun in the evening.

He pushed back the flap of the sleeping-bag and rose to his full height, passing his hands over his face, rubbing the sleep from his eyes. He was an enormous man, standing six feet two inches in his reindeer footnips and having the look more of a prize-fighter than of a scientist. Even making allowances for its coating of dirt and its harsh, black stubble of half a week's growth, the face was not pleasant. Bennett was an ugly man. His lower jaw was huge almost to deformity, like that of the bull-dog, the chin salient, the mouth close-gripped, with great lips, indomitable, brutal. The forehead was contracted and small, the forehead of men of single ideas, and the eyes, too, were small and twinkling, one of them marred by a sharply defined cast.

But as Bennett was fumbling in the tin box that was lashed upon the number four sledge, looking for his notebook wherein he had begun his calculations for latitude, he was surprised to find a copy of the record he had left in the instrument box under the cairn at Cape Kamenni at the beginning of this southerly march. He had supposed that this copy had been mislaid, and was not a little relieved to come across it now. He read it through hastily, his mind reviewing again the incidents of the last few months. Certain extracts of this record ran as follows:

Arctic steamer Freja, on ice off Cape Kamenni, New Siberian Islands, 76 deg. 10 min. north latitude, 150 deg. 40 min. east longitude, July 12, 1891. . . . We accordingly froze the ship in on the last day of September, 1890, and during the following winter drifted with the pack in a northwesterly direction. . . . On Friday, July 10, 1891, being in latitude 76 deg. 10 min. north; longitude 150 deg. 10 min. east, the Freja was caught in a severe nip between two floes and was crushed, sinking in about two hours. We abandoned her, saving 200 days' provisions and all necessary clothing, instruments, etc. . . .
I shall now attempt a southerly march over the ice to Kolyuchin Bay by way of Wrangel Island, where provisions have been cached, hoping to fall in with the relief ships or steam whalers on the way. Our party consists of the following twelve persons: . . . All well with the exception of Mr. Ferriss, the chief engineer, whose left hand has been badly frostbitten. No scurvy in the party as yet. We have eighteen Ostiak dogs with us in prime condition, and expect to drag our ship's boat upon sledges.

WARD BENNETT,
Commanding Freja Arctic Exploring Expedition.

Bennett returned this copy of the record to its place in the box, and stood for a moment in the centre of the tent, his head bent to avoid the ridge-pole, looking thoughtfully upon the ground.

Well, so far all had gone right—no scurvy, provisions in plenty. The dogs were in good condition, his men cheerful, trusting in him as in a god, and surely no leader could wish for a better lieutenant and comrade than Richard Ferriss—but this hummocky ice—these pressure-ridges which the expedition had met the day before. Instead of turning at once to his ciphering Bennett drew the hood of the wolfskin coat over his head, buttoned a red flannel mask across his face, and, raising the flap of the tent, stepped outside.

Under the lee of the tent the dogs were sleeping, moveless bundles of fur, black and white, perceptibly steaming. The three great McClintock sledges, weighted down with the Freja's boats and with the expedition's impedimenta, lay where they had been halted the evening before.

In the sky directly in front of Bennett as he issued from the tent three moons, hooped in a vast circle of nebulous light, shone roseate through a fine mist, while in the western heavens streamers of green, orange, and vermilion light, immeasurably vast, were shooting noiselessly from horizon to zenith.

But Bennett had more on his mind that morning than mock-moons and auroras. To the south and east, about a quarter of a mile from the tent, the pressure of the floes had thrown up an enormous ridge of shattered ice-cakes, a mound, a long hill of blue-green slabs and blocks huddling together at every conceivable angle. It was nearly twenty feet in height, quite the highest point that Bennett could discover. Scrambling and climbing over countless other ridges that intervened, he made his way to it, ascended it almost on hands and knees, and, standing upon its highest point, looked long and carefully to the southward.

A wilderness beyond all thought, words, or imagination desolate stretched out before him there forever and forever—ice, ice, ice, fields and floes of ice,

4

laying themselves out under that gloomy sky, league after league, endless, sombre, infinitely vast, infinitely formidable. But now it was no longer the smooth ice over which the expedition had for so long been travelling. In every direction, intersecting one another at ten thousand points, crossing and recrossing, weaving a gigantic, bewildering network of gashed, jagged, splintered ice-blocks, ran the pressure-ridges and hummocks. In places a score or more of these ridges had been wedged together to form one huge field of broken slabs of ice miles in width, miles in length. From horizon to horizon there was no level place, no open water, no pathway. The view to the southward resembled a tempest-tossed ocean suddenly frozen.

One of these ridges Bennett had just climbed, and upon it he now stood. Even for him, unencumbered, carrying no weight, the climb had been difficult; more than once he had slipped and fallen. At times he had been obliged to go forward almost on his hands and knees. And yet it was across that jungle of ice, that unspeakable tangle of blue-green slabs and cakes and blocks, that the expedition must now advance, dragging its boats, its sledges, its provisions, instruments, and baggage.

Bennett stood looking. Before him lay his task. There under his eyes was the Enemy. Face to face with him was the titanic primal strength of a chaotic world, the stupendous still force of a merciless nature, waiting calmly, waiting silently to close upon and crush him. For a long time he stood watching. Then the great brutal jaw grew more salient than ever, the teeth set and clenched behind the close-gripped lips, the cast in the small twinkling eyes grew suddenly more pronounced. One huge fist raised, and the arm slowly extended forward like the resistless moving of a piston. Then when his arm was at its full reach Bennett spoke as though in answer to the voiceless, terrible challenge of the Ice. Through his clenched teeth his words came slow and measured.

" But I'll break you, by God! believe me, I will."

After a while he returned to the tent, awoke the cook, and while breakfast was being prepared completed his calculations for latitude, wrote up his ice-journal, and noted down the temperature and the direction and velocity of the wind. As he was finishing, Richard Ferriss, who was the chief engineer and second in command, awoke and immediately asked the latitude.

" Seventy-four-fifteen," answered Bennett without looking up.

" Seventy-four-fifteen," repeated Ferriss, nodding his head; " we didn't make much distance yesterday."

" I hope we can make as much to-day," returned Bennett grimly as he put away his observation-journal and notebooks.

" How's the ice to the south'ard? "

" Bad; wake the men."

After breakfast and while the McClintocks were being loaded Bennett sent Ferriss on ahead to choose a road through and over the ridges. It was dreadful work. For two hours Ferriss wandered about amid the broken ice all but hopelessly bewildered. But at length, to his great satisfaction, he beheld a fairly open stretch about a quarter of a mile in length lying out to the southwest and not too far out of the expedition's line of march. Some dozen ridges would have to be crossed before this level was reached; but there was no help for it, so Ferriss planted his flags where the heaps of ice-blocks seemed least impracticable and returned toward the camp. It had already been broken, and on his way he met the entire expedition involved in the intricacies of the first rough ice.

All of the eighteen dogs had been harnessed to the number two sledge, that carried the whaleboat and the major part of the provisions, and every man of the party, Bennett included, was straining at the haul-ropes with the dogs. Foot by foot the sledge came over the ridge, grinding and lurching among the ice-blocks; then, partly by guiding, partly by lifting, it was piloted down the slope, only in the end to escape from all control and come crashing downward among the dogs, jolting one of the medicine chests from its lashings and butting its nose heavily against the foot of the next hummock immediately beyond. But the men scrambled to their places again, the medicine chest was replaced, and Muck Tu, the Esquimau dog-master, whipped forward his dogs. Ferriss, too, laid hold. The next hummock was surmounted, the dogs panting, and the men, even in that icy air, reeking with perspiration. Then suddenly and without the least warning Bennett and McPherson, who were in the lead, broke through some young ice into water up to their breasts, Muck Tu and one of the dogs breaking through immediately afterward. The men were pulled out, or, of their own efforts, climbed upon the ice again. But in an instant their clothes were frozen to rattling armor.

"Bear off to the east'ard, here!" commanded Bennett, shaking the icy, stinging water from his sleeves. "Everybody on the ropes now!"

Another pressure-ridge was surmounted, then a third, and by an hour after the start they had arrived at the first one of Ferriss's flags. Here the number two sledge was left, and the entire expedition, dogs and men, returned to camp to bring up the number one McClintock loaded with the Freja's cutter and with the sleeping-bags, instruments, and tent. This sledge was successfully dragged over the first two hummocks, but as it was being hauled up the third its left-hand runner suddenly buckled and turned under it with a loud snap. There was nothing for it now but to remove the entire load and to set Hawes, the carpenter, to work upon its repair.

"Up your other sledge!" ordered Bennett.

Once more the expedition returned to the morning's camping-place, and, harnessing itself to the third McClintock, struggled forward with it for an hour and a half until it was up with the first sledge and Ferriss's flag. Fortunately the two dog-sleds, four and five, were light, and Bennett, dividing his forces, brought them up in a single haul. But Hawes called out that the broken sledge was now repaired. The men turned to at once, reloaded it, and hauled it onward, so that by noon every sledge had been moved forward quite a quarter of a mile.

But now, for the moment, the men, after going

over the same ground seven times, were used up, and Muck Tu could no longer whip the dogs to their work. Bennett called a halt. Hot tea was made, and pemmican and hardtack served out.

"We'll have easier hauling this afternoon, men," said Bennett; "this next ridge is the worst of the lot; beyond that Mr. Ferriss says we've got nearly a quarter of a mile of level floes."

On again at one o'clock; but the hummock of which Bennett had spoken proved absolutely impassable for the loaded sledges. It was all one that the men lay to the ropes like draught-horses, and that Muck Tu flogged the dogs till the goad broke in his hands. The men lost their footing upon the slippery ice and fell to their knees; the dogs laid down in the traces groaning and whining. The sledge would not move.

"Unload!" commanded Bennett.

The lashings were taken off, and the loads, including the great, cumbersome whaleboat itself, carried over the hummock by hand. Then the sledge itself was hauled over and reloaded upon the other side. Thus the whole five sledges.

The work was bitter hard; the knots of the lashings were frozen tight and coated with ice; the cases of provisions, the medicine chests, the canvas bundle of sails, boat-covers, and tents unwieldy and of enormous weight; the footing on the slippery, uneven ice precarious, and more than once a man, staggering under his load, broke through the crust into water so cold that the sensation was like that of burning.

But at last everything was over, the sledges reloaded, and the forward movement resumed. Only one low hummock now intervened between them and the longed-for level floe.

However, as they were about to start forward again a lamentable gigantic sound began vibrating in their ears, a rumbling, groaning note rising by quick degrees to a strident shriek. Other sounds, hollow and shrill—treble mingling with diapason—joined in the first. The noise came from just beyond the pressure-mound at the foot of which the party had halted.

"Forward!" shouted Bennett; "hurry there, men!"

Desperately eager, the men bent panting to their work. The sledge bearing the whaleboat topped the hummock.

"Now, then, over with her!" cried Ferriss.

But it was too late. As they stood looking down upon it for an instant, the level floe, their one sustaining hope during all the day, suddenly cracked from side to side with the noise of ordnance. Then the groaning and shrieking recommenced. The crack immediately closed up, the pressure on the sides of the floe began again, and on the smooth surface of the ice, domes and mounds abruptly reared themselves. As the pressure increased these domes and mounds cracked and burst into countless blocks and slabs. Ridge after ridge was formed in the twinkling of an eye. Thundering like a cannonade of siege guns, the whole floe burst up, jagged, splintered, hummocky. In less than three minutes, and while the Freja's men stood watching, the level stretch toward which since morning they had struggled with incalculable toil was ground up into a vast mass of confused and pathless rubble.

"Oh, this will never do," muttered Ferriss, disheartened.

"Come on, men!" exclaimed Bennett. "Mr. Ferriss, go forward, and choose a road for us."

The labour of the morning was recommenced. With infinite patience, infinite hardship, the sledges one by one were advanced. So heavy were the three larger McClintocks that only one could be handled at a time, and that one taxed the combined efforts of men and dogs to the uttermost. The same ground had to be covered seven times. For every yard gained seven had to be travelled. It was not a march, it was a battle; a battle without rest and without end and without mercy; a battle with an Enemy whose power was beyond all estimate and whose movements were not reducible to any known law. A certain course would be mapped, certain plans formed, a certain objective determined, and before the course could be finished, the plans executed, or the objective point attained the perverse, inexplicable movement of the ice baffled their determination and set at naught their best ingenuity.

At four o'clock it began to snow. Since the middle of the forenoon the horizon had been obscured by clouds and mist so that no observation for position could be taken. Steadily the clouds had advanced, and by four o'clock the expedition found itself enveloped by wind and driving snow. The flags could no longer be distinguished; thin and treacherous ice was concealed under drifts; the dogs floundered helplessly; the men could scarcely open their eyes against the wind and fine, powder-like snow, and at times when they came to drag forward the last sledge they found it so nearly buried in the snow that it must be dug out before it could be moved.

Toward half past five the odometer on one of the dog-sleds registered a distance of three-quarters of a mile made since morning. Bennett called a halt, and camp was pitched in the lee of one of the larger hummocks. The alcohol cooker was set going, and supper was had under the tent, the men eating as they lay in their sleeping-bags. But even while eating they fell asleep, drooping lower and lower, finally collapsing upon the canvas floor of the tent, the food still in their mouths.

Yet, for all that, the night was miserable. Even after that day of superhuman struggle they were not to be allowed a few hours of unbroken rest. By midnight the wind had veered to the east and was blowing a gale. An hour later the tent came down. Exhausted as they were, they must turn out and wrestle with that slatting, ice-sheathed canvas, and it was not until half an hour later that everything was fast again.

Once more they crawled into the sleeping-bags, but soon the heat from their bodies melted the ice upon their clothes, and pools of water formed under each man, wetting him to the skin. Sleep was impossible. It grew colder and colder as the night advanced, and the gale increased. At three o'clock in the morning the centigrade thermometer was at eighteen degrees below. The cooker was lighted again, and until six o'clock the party huddled wretchedly about it, dozing and waking, shivering continually.

Breakfast at half past six o'clock ; under way again an hour later. There was no change in the nature of the ice. Ridge succeeded ridge, hummock followed upon hummock. The wind was going down, but the snow still fell as fine and bewildering as ever. The cold was intense. Dennison, the doctor and naturalist of the expedition, having slipped his mitten, had his hand frostbitten before he could recover it. Two of the dogs, Big Joe and Stryelka, were noticeably giving out.

But Bennett, his huge jaws clenched, his small, distorted eyes twinkling viciously through the apertures of the wind-mask, his harsh, black eyebrows lowering under the narrow, contracted forehead, drove the expedition to its work relentlessly. Not Muck Tu, the dog-master, had his Ostiaks more completely under his control than he his men. He himself did the work of three. On that vast frame of bone and muscle, fatigue seemed to leave no trace. Upon that inexorable bestial determination difficulties beyond belief left no mark. Not one of the twelve men under his command fighting the stubborn ice with tooth and nail who was not galvanised with his tremendous energy. It was as though a spur was in their flanks, a lash upon their backs. Their minds, their wills, their efforts, their physical strength to the last ounce and pennyweight belonged indissolubly to him. For the time being they were his slaves, his serfs, his beasts of burden, his draught animals, no better than the dogs straining in the traces beside them. Forward they must and would go until they dropped in the harness or he gave the word to pause.

At four o'clock in the afternoon Bennett halted. Two miles had been made since the last camp, and now human endurance could go no farther. Sometimes when the men fell they were unable to get up. It was evident there was no more in them that day.

In his ice-journal for that date Bennett wrote:

. . . Two miles covered by 4 P.M. Our course continues to be south, 20 degrees west (magnetic). The ice still hummocky. At this rate we shall be on half rations long before we reach Wrangel Island. No observation possible since day before yesterday on account of snow and clouds. Stryelka, one of our best dogs, gave out to-day. Shot him and fed him to the others. Our advance to the southwest is slow but sure, and every day brings nearer our objective. Temperature at 6 P.M., 6.8 degrees Fahr. (minus 14 degrees C.). Wind, east; force, 2.

The next morning was clear for two hours after breakfast, and when Ferriss returned from his task of path-finding he reported to Bennett that he had seen a great many water-blinks off to the southwest.

"The wind of yesterday has broken the ice up," observed Bennett; "we shall have hard work to-day."

A little after midday, at a time when they had wrested some thousand yards to the southward from the grip of the ice, the expedition came to the first lane of open water, about three hundred feet in width. Bennett halted the sledges and at once set about constructing a bridge of floating cakes of ice. But the work of keeping these ice-blocks in place long enough for the transfer of even a single sledge seemed at times to be beyond their most strenuous endeavour. The first sledge with the cutter crossed in safety. Then came the turn of number two, loaded with the provisions and whaleboat. It was two-thirds of the way across when the opposite side of the floe abruptly shifted its position, and thirty feet of open water suddenly widened out directly in front of the line of progress.

" Cut loose! " commanded Bennett upon the instant. The ice-block upon which they were gathered was set free in the current. The situation was one of the greatest peril. The entire expedition, men and dogs together, with their most important sledge, was adrift. But the oars and mast and the pole of the tent were had from the whaleboat, and little by little they ferried themselves across. The gap was bridged again and the dog-sleds transferred.

But now occurred the first real disaster since the destruction of the ship. Half-way across the crazy pontoon bridge of ice, the dogs, harnessed to one of the small sleds, became suddenly terrified. Before any one could interfere they had bolted from Muck Tu's control in a wild break for the farther side of the ice. The sled was overturned; pell-mell the dogs threw themselves into the water; the sled sank, the load-lashing parted, and two medicine chests, the bag of sewing materials—of priceless worth—a coil of wire ropes, and three hundred and fifty pounds of pemmican were lost in the twinkling of an eye.

Without comment Bennett at once addressed

himself to making the best of the business. The dogs were hauled upon the ice; the few loads that yet remained upon the sled were transferred to another; that sled was abandoned, and once more the expedition began its never-ending battle to the southward.

The lanes of open water, as foreshadowed by the water-blinks that Ferriss had noted in the morning, were frequent; alternating steadily with hummocks and pressure-ridges. But the perversity of the ice was all but heart-breaking. At every hour the lanes opened and closed. At one time in the afternoon they had arrived upon the edge of a lane wide enough to justify them in taking to their boats. The sledges were unloaded, and stowed upon the boats themselves, and oars and sails made ready. Then as Bennett was about to launch the lane suddenly closed up. What had been water became a level floe, and again the process of unloading and reloading had to be undertaken.

That evening Big Joe and two other dogs, Gavriga and Patsy, were shot because of their uselessness in the traces. Their bodies were cut up to feed their mates.

"I can spare the dogs," wrote Bennett in his journal for that day—a Sunday—"but McPherson, one of the best men of the command, gives me some uneasiness. His frozen footnips have chafed sores in his ankle. One of these has ulcerated, and the doctor tells me is in a serious condition. His pain is so great that he can no longer haul with the others. Shall relieve him from work during the morrow's march. Less than a mile covered to-day. Meridian observation for latitude impossible on account of fog. Divine services at 5:30 P.M.

A Man's Woman

A week passed, then another. There was no change, neither in the character of the ice nor in the expedition's daily routine. Their toil was incredible; at times an hour's unremitting struggle would gain but a few yards. The dogs, instead of aiding them, were rapidly becoming mere encumbrances. Four more had been killed, a fifth had been drowned, and two, wandering from camp, had never returned. The second dog-sled had been abandoned. The condition of McPherson's foot was such that no work could be demanded from him. Hawes, the carpenter, was down with fever and kept everybody awake all night by talking in his sleep. Worse than all, however, Ferriss's right hand was again frostbitten, and this time Dennison, the doctor, was obliged to amputate it above the wrist.

" . . . But I am no whit disheartened," wrote Bennett. "Succeed I must and shall."

A few days after the operation on Ferriss's hand Bennett decided it would be advisable to allow the party a full twenty-four hours' rest. The march of the day before had been harder than any they had yet experienced, and, in addition to McPherson and the carpenter, the doctor himself was upon the sick list.

In the evening Bennett and Ferriss took a long walk or rather climb over the ice to the southwest, picking out a course for the next day's march.

A great friendship, not to say affection, had sprung up between these two men, a result of their long and close intimacy on board the Freja and of

the hardships and perils they had shared during the
past few weeks while leading the expedition in the
retreat to the southward. When they had decided
upon the track of the morrow's advance they sat
down for a moment upon the crest of a hummock
to breathe themselves, their elbows on their knees,
looking off to the south over the desolation of
broken ice.

With his one good hand Ferriss drew a pipe and
a handful of tea leaves wrapped in oiled paper from
the breast of his deer-skin parkie.

"Do you mind filling this pipe for me, Ward?"
he asked of Bennett.

Bennett glanced at the tea leaves and handed
them back to Ferriss, and in answer to his remon-
strance produced a pouch of his own.

"Tobacco!" cried Ferriss, astonished; "why, I
thought we smoked our last aboard ship."

"No, I saved a little of mine."

"Oh, well," answered Ferriss, trying to interfere
with Bennett, who was filling his pipe, "I don't
want your tobacco; this tea does very well."

"I tell you I have eight-tenths of a kilo left," lied
Bennett, lighting the pipe and handing it back to
him. "Whenever you want a smoke you can set
to me."

Bennett lit a pipe of his own, and the two began
to smoke.

"'M, ah!" murmured Ferriss, drawing upon
the pipe ecstatically, "I thought I never was
going to taste good weed again till we should get
home."

Bennett said nothing. There was a long silence.

Home! what did not that word mean for them? To leave all this hideous, grisly waste of ice behind, to have done with fighting, to rest, to forget responsibility, to have no more anxiety, to be warm once more—warm and well fed and dry—to see a tree again, to rub elbows with one's fellows, to know the meaning of warm handclasps and the faces of one's friends.

"Dick," began Bennett abruptly after a long while, "if we get stuck here in this damned ice I'm going to send you and probably Metz on ahead for help. We'll make a two-man kyack for you to use when you reach the limit of the pack, but besides the kyack you'll carry nothing but your provisions, sleeping-bags, and rifle, and travel as fast as you can." Bennett paused for a moment, then in a different voice continued: "I wrote a letter last night that I was going to give you in case I should have to send you on such a journey, but I think I might as well give it to you now."

He drew from his pocket an envelope carefully wrapped in oilskin.

"If anything should happen to the expedition—to me—I want you to see that this letter is delivered."

He paused again.

"You see, Dick, it's like this; there's a girl——" his face flamed suddenly, "no—no, a woman, a grand, noble, man's woman, back in God's country who is a great deal to me—everything in fact. She don't know, hasn't a guess, that I care. I never spoke to her about it. But if anything should turn up I should want her to know how it had been with

me, how much she was to me. So I've written her.
You'll see that she gets it, will you?"

He handed the little package to Ferriss, and continued indifferently, and resuming his accustomed
manner:

"If we get as far as Wrangel Island you can give
it back to me. We are bound to meet the relief
ships or the steam whalers in that latitude. Oh,
you can look at the address," added Bennett as
Ferriss, turning the envelope bottom side up, was
thrusting it into his breast pocket; "you know her
even better than I do. It's Lloyd Searight."

Ferriss's teeth shut suddenly upon his pipe-
stem.

Bennett rose. "Tell Muck Tu," he said, "in
case I don't think of it again, that the dogs must be
fed from now on from those that die. I shall want
the dog biscuit and dried fish for our own use."

"I suppose it will come to that," answered
Ferriss.

"Come to that!" returned Bennett grimly; "I
hope the dogs themselves will live long enough for
us to eat them. And don't misunderstand," he
added; "I talk about our getting stuck in the ice,
about my not pulling through; it's only because one
must foresee everything, be prepared for everything.
Remember—I—shall—pull—through."

But that night, long after the rest were sleeping,
Ferriss, who had not closed his eyes, bestirred himself, and, as quietly as possible, crawled from his
sleeping-bag. He fancied there was some slight
change in the atmosphere, and wanted to read the
barometer affixed to a stake just outside the tent.

Yet when he had noted that it was, after all, stationary, he stood for a moment looking out across the ice with unseeing eyes. Then from a pocket in his furs he drew a little folder of morocco. It was pitiably worn, stained with sea-water, patched and repatched, its frayed edges sewed together again with ravellings of cloth and sea-grasses. Loosening with his teeth the thong of walrus-hide with which it was tied, Ferriss opened it and held it to the faint light of an aurora just paling in the northern sky.

"So," he muttered after a while, " so—Bennett, too——"

For a long time Ferriss stood looking at Lloyd's picture till the purple streamers in the north faded into the cold gray of the heavens. Then he shot a glance above him.

"God Almighty, bless her and keep her!" he prayed.

Far off, miles away, an ice-floe split with the prolonged reverberation of thunder. The aurora was gone. Ferriss returned to the tent.

The following week the expedition suffered miserably. Snowstorm followed snowstorm, the temperature dropped to twenty-two degrees below the freezing-point, and gales of wind from the east whipped and scourged the struggling men incessantly with myriad steel-tipped lashes. At night the agony in their feet was all but unbearable. It was impossible to be warm, impossible to be dry. Dennison, in a measure, recovered his health, but the ulcer on McPherson's foot had so eaten the flesh that the muscles were visible. Hawes's monotonous chatter and crazy whimperings filled the tent every night.

The only pleasures left them, the only breaks in the monotony of that life, were to eat, and, when possible, to sleep. Thought, reason, and reflection dwindled in their brains. Instincts—the primitive, elemental impulses of the animal—possessed them instead. To eat, to sleep, to be warm—they asked nothing better. The night's supper was a vision that dwelt in their imaginations hour after hour throughout the entire day. Oh, to sit about the blue flame of alcohol sputtering underneath the old and battered cooker of sheet-iron! To smell the delicious savour of the thick, boiling soup! And then the meal itself—to taste the hot, coarse, meaty food; to feel that unspeakably grateful warmth and glow, that almost divine sensation of satiety spreading through their poor, shivering bodies, and then sleep; sleep, though quivering with cold; sleep, though the wet searched the flesh to the very marrow; sleep, though the feet burned and crisped with torture; sleep, sleep, the dreamless stupefaction of exhaustion, the few hours' oblivion, the day's short armistice from pain!

But stronger, more insistent than even these instincts of the animal was the blind, unreasoned impulse that set their faces to the southward: "To get forward, to get forward." Answering the resistless influence of their leader, that indomitable man of iron whom no fortune could break nor bend, and who imposed his will upon them as it were a yoke of steel—this idea became for them a sort of obsession. Forward, if it were only a yard; if it were only a foot. Forward over the heart-breaking, rubble ice; forward against the biting, shrieking wind; forward in the face of the blinding snow; forward through the brittle crusts and icy water; forward, although every step was an agony, though the haul-rope cut like a dull knife, though their clothes were sheets of ice. Blinded, panting, bruised, bleeding, and exhausted, dogs and men, animals all, the expedition struggled forward.

One day, a little before noon, while lunch was being cooked, the sun broke through the clouds, and for upward of half an hour the ice-pack was one blinding, diamond glitter. Bennett ran for his sextant and got an observation, the first that had been possible for nearly a month. He worked out their latitude that same evening.

The next morning Ferriss was awakened by a touch on his shoulder. Bennett was standing over him.

"Come outside here a moment," said Bennett in a low voice. "Don't wake the men."

"Did you get our latitude?" asked Ferriss as the two came out of the tent.

"Yes, that's what I want to tell you."

"What is it?"

"Seventy-four-nineteen."

"Why, what do you mean?" asked Ferriss quickly.

"Just this: That the ice-pack we're on is drifting faster to the north than we are marching to the south. We are farther north now than we were a month ago for all our marching."

II.

By eleven o'clock at night the gale had increased to such an extent and the sea had begun to build so high that it was a question whether or not the whaleboat would ride the storm. Bennett finally decided that it would be impossible to reach the land—stretching out in a long, dark blur to the southwest —that night, and that the boat must run before the wind if he was to keep her afloat. The number two cutter, with Ferriss in command, was a bad sailer, and had fallen astern. She was already out of hailing distance; but Bennett, who was at the whaleboat's tiller, in the instant's glance that he dared to shoot behind him saw with satisfaction that Ferriss had followed his example.

The whaleboat and the number two cutter were the only boats now left to the expedition. The third boat had been abandoned long before they had reached open water.

An hour later Adler, the sailing-master, who had been bailing, and who sat facing Bennett, looked back through the storm; then, turning to Bennett, said:

" Beg pardon, sir, I think they are signalling us."

Bennett did not answer, but, with his hand gripping the tiller, kept his face to the front, his glance alternating between the heaving prow of the boat and the huge gray billows hissing with froth careering rapidly alongside. To pause for a moment, to vary by ever so little from the course of the storm, might mean the drowning of them all. After a few moments Adler spoke again, touching his cap.

"I'm sure I see a signal, sir."

"No, you don't," answered Bennett.

"Beg pardon, I'm quite sure I do."

Bennett leaned toward him, the cast in his eyes twinkling with a wicked light, the furrow between the eyebrows deepening. "I tell you, you don't see any signal; do you understand? You don't see any signal until I choose to have you."

The night was bitter hard for the occupants of the whaleboat. In their weakened condition they were in no shape to fight a polar hurricane in an open boat.

For three weeks they had not known the meaning of full rations. During the first days after the line of march over the ice had been abruptly changed to the west in the hope of reaching open water, only three-quarter rations had been issued, and now for the last two days half rations had been their portion. The gnawing of hunger had begun. Every man was perceptibly weaker. Matters were getting desperate.

But by seven o'clock the next morning the storm had blown itself out. To Bennett's inexpressible relief the cutter hove in view. Shaping their course to landward once more, the boats kept company, and by the middle of the afternoon Bennett and the crew of the whaleboat successfully landed upon a bleak, desolate, and wind-scourged coast. But in some way, never afterward sufficiently explained, the cutter under Ferriss's command was crushed in the floating ice within one hundred yards of the shore. The men and stores were landed—the water being shallow enough for wading—but the boat was a hopeless wreck.

"I believe it's Cape Shelaski," said Bennett to Ferriss when camp had been made and their maps consulted. "But if it is, it's charted thirty-five minutes too far to the west."

Before breaking camp the next morning Bennett left this record under a cairn of rocks upon the highest point of the cape, further marking the spot by one of the boat's flags:

The Freja Arctic Exploring Expedition landed at this point October 28, 1891. Our ship was nipped and sunk in 76 deg. 10 min. north latitude on the 12th of July last. I then attempted a southerly march to Wrangel Island, but found such a course impracticable on account of northerly drift of ice. On the 1st of October I accordingly struck off to the westward to find open water at the limit of the ice, being compelled to abandon one boat and two sledges on the way. A second boat was crushed beyond repair in drifting ice while attempting a landing at this place. Our one remaining boat being too small to accommodate the members of the expedition, circumstances oblige me to begin an overland march toward Kolyuchin Bay, following the line of the coast. We expect either to winter among the Chuckch settlements mentioned by Nordenskjold as existing upon the eastern shores of Kolyuchin Bay or to fall in with the relief ships or the steam whalers en route. By issuing half rations I have enough provisions for eighteen days, and have saved all records, observations, papers, instruments, etc. Enclosed is the muster roll of the expedition. No scurvy as yet and no deaths. Our sick are William Hawes, carpenter, arctic fever, serious; David McPherson, seaman, ulceration of left foot, serious. The general condition of the rest of the men is fair, though much weakened by exposure and lack of food.

(Signed)   WARD BENNETT,
                                    Commanding.

But during the night, their first night on land, Bennett resolved upon a desperate expedient. Not only the boat was to be abandoned, but also the sledges, and not only the sledges, but every article of weight not absolutely necessary to the existence of the party. Two weeks before, the sun had set not to rise again for six months. Winter was upon them and darkness. The Enemy was drawing near. The great remorseless grip of the Ice was closing. It was no time for half-measures and hesitation; now it was life or death.

The sense of their peril, the nearness of the Enemy, strung Bennett's nerves taut as harp-strings. His will hardened to the flinty hardness of the ice itself. His strength of mind and of body seemed suddenly to quadruple itself. His determination was that of the battering-ram, blind, deaf, resistless. The ugly set of his face became all the more ugly, the contorted eyes flashing, the great jaw all but simian. He appeared physically larger. It was no longer a man; it was a giant, an ogre, a colossal jotun hurling ice-blocks, fighting out a battle unspeakable, in the dawn of the world, in chaos and in darkness.

The impedimenta of the expedition were broken up into packs that each man carried upon his shoulders. From now on everything that hindered the rapidity of their movements must be left behind.

A Man's Woman

Six dogs (all that remained of the pack of eighteen) still accompanied them.

Bennett had hoped and had counted upon his men for an average daily march of sixteen miles, but the winter gales driving down from the northeast beat them back; the ice and snow that covered the land were no less uneven than the hummocks of the pack. All game had migrated far to the southward.

Every day the men grew weaker and weaker; their provisions dwindled. Again and again one or another of them, worn out beyond human endurance, would go to sleep while marching and would fall to the ground.

Upon the third day of this overland march one of the dogs suddenly collapsed upon the ground, exhausted and dying. Bennett had ordered such of the dogs that gave out cut up and their meat added to the store of the party's provisions. Ferriss and Muck Tu had started to pick up the dead dog when the other dogs, famished and savage, sprang upon their fallen mate. The two men struck and kicked, all to no purpose; the dogs turned upon them snarling and snapping. They, too, demanded to live; they, too, wanted to be fed. It was a hideous business. There in that half-night of the polar circle, lost and forgotten on a primordial shore, back into the stone age once more, men and animals fought one another for the privilege of eating a dead dog.

But their life was not all inhuman; Bennett at least could rise even above humanity, though his men must perforce be dragged so far below it. At the end of the first week Hawes, the carpenter, died.

A Man's Woman

When they awoke in the morning he was found motionless and stiff in his sleeping-bag. Some sort of grave was dug, the poor racked body lowered into it, and before it was filled with snow and broken ice Bennett, standing quietly in the midst of the bare-headed group, opened his prayer-book and began with the tremendous words, " I am the Resurrection and the Life——"

It was the beginning of the end. A week later the actual starvation began. Slower and slower moved the expedition on its daily march, faltering, staggering, blinded and buffeted by the incessant northeast winds, cruel, merciless, keen as knife-blades. Hope long since was dead; resolve wore thin under friction of disaster; like a rat, hunger gnawed at them hour after hour; the cold was one unending agony. Still Bennett was unbroken, still he urged them forward. For so long as they could move he would drive them on.

Toward four o'clock on the afternoon of one particularly hard day, word was passed forward to Bennett at the head of the line that something was wrong in the rear.

" It's Adler; he's down again and can't get up; asks you to leave him."

Bennett halted the line and went back some little distance to find Adler lying prone upon his back, his eyes half closed, breathing short and fast. He shook him roughly by the shoulder.

" Up with you! "

Adler opened his eyes and shook his head.

" I—I'm done for this time, sir; just leave me here—please."

"H'up!" shouted Bennett; "you're not done for; I know better."

"Really, sir, I—I *can't*."

"H'up!"

"If you would only please—for God's sake, sir. It's more than I'm made for."

Bennett kicked him in the side.

"H'up with you!"

Adler struggled to his feet again, Bennett aiding him.

"Now, then, can you go five yards?"

"I think—I don't know—perhaps——"

"Go them, then."

The other moved forward.

"Can you go five more; answer, speak up, can you?"

Adler nodded his head.

"Go them—and another five—and another—there—that's something like a man, and let's have no more woman's drivel about dying."

"But——"

Bennett came close to him, shaking a forefinger in his face, thrusting forward his chin wickedly.

"My friend, I'll drive you like a dog, but," his fist clenched in the man's face, "I'll *make* you pull through."

Two hours later Adler finished the day's march at the head of the line.

The expedition began to eat its dogs. Every evening Bennett sent Muck Tu and Adler down to the shore to gather shrimps, though fifteen hundred of these shrimps hardly filled a gill measure. The party chewed reindeer-moss growing in scant patches in the snow-buried rocks, and at times made a thin, sickly infusion from the arctic willow. Again and again Bennett despatched the Esquimau and Clarke, the best shots in the party, on hunting expeditions to the southward. Invariably they returned empty-handed. Occasionally they reported old tracks of reindeer and foxes, but the winter colds had driven everything far inland. Once only Clarke shot a snow-bunting, a little bird hardly bigger than a sparrow. Still Bennett pushed forward.

One morning in the beginning of the third week, after a breakfast of two ounces of dog meat and a half cup of willow tea, Ferriss and Bennett found themselves a little apart from the others. The men were engaged in lowering the tent. Ferriss glanced behind to be assured he was out of hearing, then:

" How about McPherson? " he said in a low voice.

McPherson's foot was all but eaten to the bone by now. It was a miracle how the man had kept up thus far. But at length he had begun to fall behind; every day he straggled more and more, and the previous evening had reached camp nearly an hour after the tent had been pitched. But he was a plucky fellow, of sterner stuff than the sailing-master, Adler, and had no thought of giving up.

Bennett made no reply to Ferriss, and the chief engineer did not repeat the question. The day's march began; almost at once breast-high snowdrifts were encountered, and when these had been left behind the expedition involved itself upon the precipitate slopes of a huge talus of ice and bare, black slabs of basalt. Fully two hours were spent in clambering over this obstacle, and on its top Bennett halted to breathe the men. But when they started forward again it was found that McPherson could not keep his feet. When he had fallen, Adler and Dennison had endeavoured to lift him, but they themselves were so weak that they, too, fell. Dennison could not rise of his own efforts, and instead of helping McPherson had to be aided himself. Bennett came forward, put an arm about McPherson, and hauled him to an upright position. The man took a step forward, but his left foot immediately doubled under him, and he came to the ground again. Three times this manœuvre was repeated; so far from marching, McPherson could not even stand.

"If I could have a day's rest——" began McPherson, unsteadily. Bennett cast a glance at Dennison, the doctor. Dennison shook his head. The foot, the entire leg below the knee, should have been amputated days ago. A month's rest even in a hospital at home would have benefited McPherson nothing.

For the fraction of a minute Bennett debated the question, then he turned to the command.

"Forward, men!"

"What—wh——" began McPherson, sitting upon the ground, looking from one face to another, bewildered, terrified. Some of the men began to move off.

"Wait—wait," exclaimed the cripple, "I—I can get along—I——" He rose to his knees, made a great effort to regain his footing, and once more came crashing down upon the ice.

" Forward ! "

" But—but—but——   *Oh, you're not going to leave me, sir ?* "

" Forward ! "

" He's been my chum, sir, all through the voyage," said one of the men, touching his cap to Bennett; " I had just as soon be left with him. I'm about done myself."

Another joined in :

" I'll stay, too—I can't leave—it's—it's too terrible."

There was a moment's hesitation. Those who had begun to move on halted. The whole expedition wavered.

Bennett caught the dog-whip from Muck Tu's hand. His voice rang like the alarm of a trumpet.

" Forward ! "

Once more Bennett's discipline prevailed. His iron hand shut down upon his men, more than ever resistless. Obediently they turned their faces to the southward. The march was resumed.

Another day passed, then two. Still the expedition struggled on. With every hour their sufferings increased. It did not seem that anything human could endure such stress and yet survive. Toward three o'clock in the morning of the third night Adler woke Bennett.

" It's Clarke, sir; he and I sleep in the same bag. I think he's going, sir."

One by one the men in the tent were awakened, and the train-oil lamp was lit.

Clarke lay in his sleeping-bag unconscious, and at long intervals drawing a faint, quick breath. The doctor bent over him, feeling his pulse, but shook his head hopelessly.

" He's dying—quietly—exhaustion from starvation."

A few moments later Clarke began to tremble slightly, the mouth opened wide; a faint rattle came from the throat.

Four miles was as much as could be made good the next day, and this though the ground was comparatively smooth. Ferriss was continually falling. Dennison and Metz were a little light-headed, and Bennett at one time wondered if Ferriss himself had absolute control of his wits. Since morning the wind had been blowing strongly in their faces. By noon it had increased. At four o'clock a violent gale was howling over the reaches of ice and rock-ribbed land. It was impossible to go forward while it lasted. The stronger gusts fairly carried their feet from under them. At half-past four the party halted. The gale was now a hurricane. The expedition paused, collected itself, went forward; halted again, again attempted to move, and came at last to a definite standstill in whirling snow-clouds and blinding, stupefying blasts.

" Pitch the tent! " said Bennett quietly. " We must wait now till it blows over."

In the lee of a mound of ice-covered rock some hundred yards from the coast the tent was pitched, and supper, such as it was, eaten in silence. All knew what this enforced halt must mean for them. That supper—each man could hold his portion in the hollow of one hand—was the last of their regular provisions. March they could not. What now?

A Man's Woman

Before crawling into their sleeping-bags, **and at** Bennett's request, all joined in repeating the Creed and the Lord's Prayer.

The next day passed, and the next, and the next. The gale continued steadily. The southerly march was discontinued. All day and all night the men kept in the tent, huddled in the sleeping-bags, sometimes sleeping eighteen and twenty hours out of the twenty-four. They lost all consciousness of the lapse of time; sensation even of suffering left them; the very hunger itself had ceased to gnaw. Only Bennett and Ferriss seemed to keep their heads. Then slowly the end began.

For that last week Bennett's entries in his ice-journal were as follows:

November 29th—Monday—Camped at 4:30 P.M. about 100 yards from the coast. Open water to the eastward as far as I can see. If I had not been compelled to abandon my boats—but it is useless to repine. I must look our situation squarely in the face. At noon served out last beef-extract, which we drank with some willow tea. Our remaining provisions consist of four-fifteenths of a pound of pemmican per man, and the rest of the dog meat. Where are the relief ships? We should at least have met the steam whalers long before this.

November 30th—Tuesday—The doctor amputated Mr. Ferriss's other hand to-day. Living gale of wind from northeast. Impossible to march against it in our weakened condition; must camp here till it abates. Made soup of the last of the dog meat this afternoon. Our last pemmican gone.

December 1st—Wednesday—Everybody getting weaker. Metz breaking down. Sent Adler down to the shore to gather shrimps. We had about a mouthful apiece for lunch. Supper, a spoonful of glycerine and hot water.

December 2d—Thursday—Metz died during the night.

35

A Man's Woman

Hansen dying. Still blowing a gale from the northeast. A hard night.

December 3d—Friday—Hansen died during early morning. Muck Tu shot a ptarmigan. Made soup. Dennison breaking down.

December 4th—Saturday—Buried Hansen under slabs of ice. Spoonful of glycerine and hot water at noon.

December 5th—Sunday—Dennison found dead this morning between Adler and myself. Too weak to bury him, or even carry him out of the tent. He must lie where he is. Divine services at 5:30 P.M. Last spoonful of glycerine and hot water.

The next day was Monday, and at some indeterminate hour of the twenty-four, though whether it was night or noon he could not say, Ferriss woke in his sleeping-bag and raised himself on an elbow, and for a moment sat stupidly watching Bennett writing in his journal. Noticing that he was awake, Bennett looked up from the page and spoke in a voice thick and muffled because of the swelling of his tongue.

"How long has this wind been blowing, Ferriss?"

"Since a week ago to-day," answered the other.

Bennett continued his writing.

. . . Incessant gales of wind for over a week. Impossible to move against them in our weakened condition. But to stay here is to perish. God help us. It is the end of everything.

Bennett drew a line across the page under the last entry, and, still holding the book in his hand, gazed slowly about the tent.

There were six of them left—five huddled together in that miserable tent—the sixth, Adler, being down on the shore gathering shrimps. In the strange and gloomy half-light that filled the tent these survivors of the Freja looked less like men than beasts. Their hair and beards were long, and seemed one with the fur covering of their bodies. Their faces were absolutely black with dirt, and their limbs were monstrously distended and fat—fat as things bloated and swollen are fat. It was the abnormal fatness of starvation, the irony of misery, the huge joke that arctic famine plays upon those whom it afterward destroys. The men moved about at times on their hands and knees; their tongues were distended, round, and slate-coloured, like the tongues of parrots, and when they spoke they bit them helplessly.

Near the flap of the tent lay the swollen dead body of Dennison. Two of the party dozed inert and stupefied in their sleeping-bags. Muck Tu was in the corner of the tent boiling his sealskin footnips over the sheet-iron cooker. Ferriss and Bennett sat on opposite sides of the tent, Bennett using his knee as a desk, Ferriss trying to free himself from the sleeping-bag with the stumps of his arms. Upon one of these stumps, the right one, a tin spoon had been lashed.

The tent was full of foul smells. The smell of drugs and of mouldy gunpowder, the smell of dirty rags, of unwashed bodies, the smell of stale smoke, of scorching sealskin, of soaked and rotting canvas that exhaled from the tent cover—every smell but that of food.

Outside the unleashed wind yelled incessantly,

like a sabbath of witches, and spun about the pitiful
shelter and went rioting past, leaping and somersaulting from rock to rock, tossing handfuls of dry,
dust-like snow into the air; folly-stricken, insensate,
an enormous, mad monster gambolling there in
some hideous dance of death, capricious, head-
strong, pitiless as a famished wolf.

In front of the tent and over a ridge of barren
rocks was an arm of the sea dotted with blocks of ice
moving silently and swiftly onward; while back
from the coast, and back from the tent and to the
south and to the west and to the east, stretched the
illimitable waste of land, rugged, gray, harsh; snow
and ice and rock, rock and ice and snow, stretching
away there under the sombre sky forever and forever; gloomy, untamed, terrible, an empty region—
the scarred battlefield of chaotic forces, the savage
desolation of a prehistoric world.

" Where's Adler? " asked Ferriss.

" He's away after shrimps," responded Bennett.

Bennett's eyes returned to his journal and rested
on the open page thoughtfully.

" Do you know what I've just written here, Ferriss? " he asked, adding without waiting for an
answer: " I've written ' It's the end of everything.' "

" I suppose it is," admitted Ferriss, looking about
the tent.

" Yes, the end of everything. It's come—at last.
. . . Well." There was a long silence. One
of the men in the sleeping-bags groaned and turned
upon his face. Outside the wind lapsed suddenly
to a prolonged sigh of infinite sadness, clamouring
again upon the instant.

A Man's Woman

"Dick," said Bennett, returning his journal to the box of records, "it *is* the end of everything, and just because it is I want to talk to you—to ask you something."

Ferriss came nearer. The horrid shouting of the wind deadened the sound of their voices; the others could not hear, and by now it would have mattered very little to any of them if they had.

"Dick," began Bennett, "nothing makes much difference now. In a few hours we shall all be like Dennison here;" he tapped the body of the doctor, who had died during the night. It was already frozen so hard that his touch upon it resounded as if it had been a log of wood. "We shall be like this pretty soon. But before—well, while I can, I want to ask you something about Lloyd Searight. You've known her all your life, and you saw her later than I did before we left. You remember I had to come to the ship two days before you, about the bilge pumps."

While Bennett had been speaking Ferriss had been sitting very erect upon his sleeping-bag, drawing figures and vague patterns in the fur of his deerskin coat with the tip of the tin spoon. Yes, Bennett was right; he, Ferriss, had known her all his life, and it was no doubt because of this very fact that she had come to be so dear to him. But he had not always known it, had never discovered his love for her until the time was at hand to say good-bye, to leave her for this mad dash for the Pole. It had been too late to speak then, and Ferriss had never told her. She was never to know that he too—like Bennett—cared.

A Man's Woman

"It seems rather foolish," continued Bennett clumsily, "but if I thought she had ever cared for me—in that way—why, it would make this that is coming to us seem—I don't know—easier to be borne perhaps. I say it very badly, but it would not be so hard to die if I thought she had ever loved me—a bit."

Ferriss was thinking very fast. Why was it he had never guessed something like this? But in Ferriss's mind the idea of the love of a woman had never associated itself with Bennett, that great, harsh man of colossal frame, so absorbed in his huge projects, so welded to his single aim, furthering his purposes to the exclusion of every other thought, desire, or emotion. Bennett was a man's man. But here Ferriss checked himself. Bennett himself had called her a man's woman, a grand, splendid man's woman. He was right; he was right. She was no less than that; small wonder, after all, that Bennett had been attracted to her. What a pair they were, strong, masterful both, insolent in the consciousness of their power!

"You have known her so well and for so long," continued Bennett, "that I am sure she must have said something to you about me. Tell me, did she ever say anything—or not that—but imply in her manner, give you to understand that she would have married me if I had asked her?"

Ferriss found time, even in such an hour, to wonder at the sudden and unexpected break in the uniform hardness of Bennett's character. Ferriss knew him well by now. Bennett was not a man to ask concessions, to catch at small favours. What he wanted he took with an iron hand, without ruth and without scruple. But in the unspeakable dissolution in which they were now involved did anything make a difference? The dreadful mill in which they had been ground had crushed from them all petty distinctions of personality, individuality. Humanity—the elements of character common to all men—only remained.

But Ferriss was puzzled as to how he should answer Bennett. On the one hand was the woman he•loved, and on the other Bennett, his best friend, his chief, his hero. They, too, had lived together for so long, had fought out the fight with the Enemy shoulder to shoulder, had battled with the same dangers, had dared the same sufferings, had undergone the same defeats and disappointments.

Ferriss felt himself in grievous straits. Must he tell Bennett the truth? Must this final disillusion be added to that long train of others, the disasters, the failures, the disappointments, and deferred hopes of all those past months? Must Bennett die hugging to his heart this bitterness as well?

"I sometimes thought," observed Bennett with a weak smile, "that she did care a little. I've surely seen something like that in her eyes at certain moments. I wish I had spoken. Did she ever say anything to you? Do you think she would have married me if I had asked her?" He paused, waiting for an answer.

"Oh—yes," hazarded Ferriss, driven to make some sort of response, hoping to end the conversation; "yes, I think she would."

"You do?" said Bennett quickly. "You think

she would? What did she say? Did she ever say anything to you?"

The thing was too cruel; Ferriss shrank from it. But suddenly an idea occurred to him. Did anything make any difference now? Why not tell his friend that which he wanted to hear, even if it were not the truth? After all that Bennett had suffered why could he not die content at least in this? What did it matter if he spoke? Did anything matter at such a time when they were all to die within the next twenty-four hours? Bennett was looking straight into his eyes; there was no time to think of consequences. Consequences? But there were to be *no* consequences. This was the end. Yet could Ferriss make Bennett receive such an untruth? Ferriss did not believe that Lloyd cared for Bennett; knew that she did not, in fact, and if she had cared, did Bennett think for an instant that she—of all women —would have confessed the fact, confessed it to him, Bennett's most intimate friend? Ferriss had known Lloyd well for a long time, had at last come to love her. But could he himself tell whether or no Lloyd cared for him? No, he could not, certainly he could not.

Meanwhile Bennett was waiting for his answer. Ferriss's mind was all confused. He could no longer distinguish right from wrong. If the lie would make Bennett happier in this last hour of his life, why not tell the lie?

"Yes," answered Ferriss, "she did say something once."

"She did?"

"Yes," continued Ferriss slowly, trying to invent

the most plausible lie. " We had been speaking of the expedition and of you. I don't know how the subject was brought up, but it came in very naturally at length. She said—yes, I recall it. She said: ' You must bring him back to me. Remember he is everything to me—everything in the world.' "

" She——" Bennett cleared his throat, then tugged at his mustache; " she said that? "

Ferriss nodded.

" Ah! " said Bennett with a quick breath, then he added: " I'm glad of that; you haven't any idea how glad I am, Dick—in spite of everything."

" Oh, yes, I guess I have," murmured Ferriss.

" No, no, indeed, you haven't," returned the other. " One has to love a woman like that, Dick, and have her—and find out—and have things come right, to appreciate it. She would have been my wife after all. I don't know how to thank you, Dick. Congratulate me."

He rose, holding out his hand; Ferriss feebly rose, too, and instinctively extended his arm, but withdrew it suddenly. Bennett paused abruptly, letting his hand fall to his side, and the two men remained there an instant, looking at the stumps of Ferriss's arms, the tin spoon still lashed to the right wrist.

A few hours later Bennett noted that the gale had begun perceptibly to abate. By afternoon he was sure that the storm would be over. As he turned to re-enter the tent after reading the wind-gauge he noted that Kamiska, their one remaining dog, had come back, and was sitting on a projection of ice a little distance away, uncertain as to her reception after her absence. Bennett was persuaded that Kamiska had not run away. Of all the Ostiaks she had been the most faithful. Bennett chose to believe that she had wandered from the tent and had lost herself in the blinding snow. But here was food. Kamiska could be killed; life could be prolonged a day or two, perhaps three, while the strongest man of the party, carrying the greater portion of the dog meat on his shoulders, could push forward and, perhaps, after all, reach Kolyuchin Bay and the Chuckch settlements and return with aid. But who could go? Assuredly not Ferriss, so weak he could scarcely keep on his feet; not Adler, who at times was delirious, and who needed the discipline of a powerful leader to keep him to his work; Muck Tu, the Esquimau, could not be trusted with the lives of all of them, and the two remaining men were in all but a dying condition. Only one man of them all was equal to the task, only one of them who still retained his strength of body and mind; he himself, Bennett. Yes, but to abandon his men?

He crawled into the tent again to get the rifle with which to shoot the dog, but, suddenly possessed of an idea, paused for a moment, seated on the sleeping-bag, his head in his hands.

Beaten? Was he beaten at last? Had the Enemy conquered. Had the Ice enclosed him in its vast, remorseless grip? Then once more his determination grew big within him, for a last time that iron will rose up in mighty protest of defeat. No, no, no; he was not beaten; he would live; he, the strongest, the fittest, would survive. Was it not right that the mightiest should live? Was it not the great law of nature? He knew himself to be strong enough to move; to march, perhaps, for two whole days; and now food had come to them, to him. Yes; but to abandon his men?

He had left McPherson, it is true; but then the lives of all of them had been involved—one life against eleven. Now he was thinking only of himself. But Ferriss—no, he could not leave Ferriss. Ferriss would come with him. They would share the dog meat between them—the whole of it. He, with Ferriss, would push on. He would reach Kolyuchin Bay and the settlements. He would be saved; he would reach home; would come back—come back to Lloyd, who loved him. Yes, but to abandon his men?

Then Bennett's great fist closed, closed and smote heavily upon his knee.

" No," he said decisively.

He had spoken his thoughts aloud, and Ferriss, who had crawled into his sleeping-bag again, looked at him curiously. Even Muck Tu turned his head from the sickening mess reeking upon the cooker. There was a noise of feet at the flap of the tent.

" It's Adler," muttered Ferriss.

Adler tore open the flap.

Then he shouted to Bennett: " Three steam whalers off the foot of the floe, sir; boat putting off! What orders, sir? "

Bennett looked at him stupidly, as yet without definite thought.

" What did you say? "

The men in the sleeping-bags, roused by Adler's shout, sat up and listened stolidly.

"Steam whalers?" said Bennett slowly. "Where? I guess not," he added, shaking his head.

Adler was swaying in his place with excitement.

"Three whalers," he repeated, "close in. They've put off—oh, my God! Listen to that."

The unmistakable sound of a steamer's whistle, raucous and prolonged, came to their ears from the direction of the coast. One of the men broke into a feeble cheer. The whole tent was rousing up. Again and again came the hoarse, insistent cry of the whistle.

"What orders, sir?" repeated Adler.

A clamour of voices filled the tent.

Ferriss came quickly up to Bennett, trying to make himself heard.

"Listen!" he cried with eager intentness, "what I told you—a while ago—about Lloyd—I thought —it's all a mistake, you don't understand——"

Bennett was not listening.

"What orders, sir?" exclaimed Adler for the third time.

Bennett drew himself up.

"My compliments to the officer in command. Tell him there are six of us left—tell him—oh, tell him anything you damn please. Men," he cried, his harsh face suddenly radiant, "make ready to get out of this! We're going home, going home to those who love us, men."

III.

As Lloyd Searight turned into Calumet Square on her way from the bookseller's, with her purchases under her arm, she was surprised to notice a drop of rain upon the back of one of her white gloves. She looked up quickly; the sun was gone. On the east side of the square, under the trees, the houses that at this hour of the afternoon should have been overlaid with golden light were in shadow. The heat that had been palpitating through all the City's streets since early morning was swiftly giving place to a certain cool and odorous dampness. There was even a breeze beginning to stir in the tops of the higher elms. As the drops began to thicken upon the warm, sun-baked asphalt under foot Lloyd sharply quickened her pace. But the summer storm was coming up rapidly. By the time she reached the great granite-built agency on the opposite side of the square she was all but running, and as she put her key in the door the rain swept down with a prolonged and muffled roar.

She let herself into the spacious, airy hallway of the agency, shutting the door by leaning against it, and stood there for an instant to get her breath. Rownie, the young mulatto girl, one of the servants of the house, who was going upstairs with an arm- ful of clean towels, turned about at the closing of the door and called:

" Jus' in time, Miss Lloyd; jus' in time. I reckon
Miss Wakeley and Miss Esther Thielman going
to get for sure wet. They ain't neither one of 'em
took ary umberel."

" Did Miss Wakeley and Miss Thielman both go
out? " demanded Lloyd quickly. " Did they both
go on a call? "

" Yes, Miss Lloyd," answered Rownie. " I don't
know because why Miss Wakeley went, but Miss
Esther Thielman got a typhoid call—another one.
That's three f'om this house come next Sunday
week. I reckon Miss Wakeley going out meks you
next on call, Miss Lloyd."

While Rownie had been speaking Lloyd had
crossed the hall to where the roster of the nurses'
names, in little movable slides, hung against the
wall. As often as a nurse was called out she removed her name from the top of this list and slid it
into place at the bottom, so that whoever found her
name at the top of the roster knew that she was
" next on call " and prepared herself accordingly.

Lloyd's name was now at the top of the list. She
had not been gone five minutes from the agency, and
it was rare for two nurses to be called out in so
short a time.

" Is it your tu'n? " asked Rownie as Lloyd faced
quickly about.

" Yes, yes," answered Lloyd, running up the
stairs, adding, as she passed the mulatto: " There's
been no call sent in since Miss Thielman left, has
there, Rownie? " Rownie shook her head.

Lloyd went directly to her room, tossed her books
aside without removing the wrappers, and set about

packing her satchel. When this was done she changed her tailor-made street dress and crisp skirt for clothes that would not rustle when she moved, and put herself neatly to rights, stripping off her rings and removing the dog-violets from her waist. Then she went to the round, old-fashioned mirror that hung between the windows of her room, and combed back her hair in a great roll from her forehead and temples, and stood there a moment or so when she had done, looking at her reflection.

She was tall and of a very vigorous build, full-throated, deep-chested, with large, strong hands and solid, round wrists. Her face was rather serious; one did not expect her to smile easily; the eyes dull blue, with no trace of sparkle and set deep under heavy, level eyebrows. Her mouth was the mouth of the obstinate, of the strong-willed, and her chin was not small. But her hair was a veritable glory, a dull-red flame, that bore back from her face in one great solid roll, dull red, like copper or old bronze, thick, heavy, almost gorgeous in its sombre radiance. Dull-red hair, dull-blue eyes, and a faint, dull glow forever on her cheeks, Lloyd was a beautiful woman; much about her that was regal, for she was very straight as well as very tall, and could look down upon most women and upon not a few men.

Lloyd turned from the mirror, laying down the comb. She had yet to pack her nurse's bag, or, since this was always ready, to make sure that none of its equipment was lacking She was very proud of this bag, as she had caused it to be made after her own ideas and design. It was of black russia leather and in the form of an ordinary valise, but set off with a fine silver clasp bearing her name and the agency's address. She brought it from the closet and ran over its contents, murmuring the while to herself:

"Clinical thermometer — brandy — hypodermic syringe—vial of oxalic-acid crystals—minim-glass —temperature charts; yes, yes, everything right."

While she was still speaking Miss Douglass, the fever nurse, knocked at her door, and, finding it ajar, entered without further ceremony.

"Are you in, Miss Searight?" called Miss Douglass, looking about the room, for Lloyd had returned to the closet and was busy washing the minim-glass.

"Yes, yes," cried Lloyd, "I am. Sit down."

"Rownie told me you are next on call," said the other, dropping on Lloyd's couch.

"So I am; I was very nearly caught, too. I ran over across the square for five minutes, and while I was gone Miss Wakeley and Esther Thielman were called. My name is at the top now."

"Esther got a typhoid case from Dr. Pitts. Do you know, Lloyd, that's—let me see, that's four— seven—nine—that's ten typhoid cases in the City that I can think of right now."

"It's everywhere; yes, I know," answered Lloyd, coming out of the room, carefully drying the minim-glass.

"We are going to have trouble with it," continued the fever nurse; "plenty of it before cool weather comes. It's almost epidemic."

Lloyd held the minim-glass against the light, scrutinising it with narrowed lids.

"What did Esther say when she knew it was an

infectious case?" she asked. "Did she hesitate
at all?"

"Not she!" declared Miss Douglass. "She's no
Harriet Freeze."

Lloyd did not answer. This case of Harriet
Freeze was one that the nurses of the house had
never forgotten and would never forgive. Miss
Freeze, a young English woman, newly graduated,
suddenly called upon to nurse a patient stricken with
smallpox, had flinched and had been found wanting
at the crucial moment, had discovered an excuse for
leaving her post, having once accepted it. It was
cowardice in the presence of the Enemy. Anything
could have been forgiven but that. On the girl's
return to the agency nothing was said, no action
taken, but for all that she was none the less expelled dishonourably from the midst of her companions. Nothing could have been stronger than the
esprit de corps of this group of young women, whose
lives were devoted to an unending battle with disease.

Lloyd continued the overhauling of her equipment, and began ruling forms for nourishment
charts, while Miss Douglass importuned her to sub-
scribe to a purse the nurses were making up for an
old cripple dying of cancer. Lloyd refused.

"You know very well, Miss Douglass, that I only
give to charity through the association."

"I know," persisted the other, "and I know you
give twice as much as all of us put together, but
with this poor old fellow it's different. We know
all about him, and every one of us in the house has
given something. You are the only one that won't,

Lloyd, and I had so hoped I could make it up to fifty dollars."

" No."

" We need only three dollars now. We can buy that little cigar stand for him for fifty dollars."

" No."

" And you won't give us just three dollars? "

" No."

" Well, you give half and I'll give half," said Miss Douglass.

" Do you think it's a question of money with me? " Lloyd smiled.

Indeed this was a poor argument with which to move Lloyd—Lloyd whose railroad stock alone brought her some fifteen thousand dollars a year.

" Well, no; I don't mean that, of course, but, Lloyd, do let us have three dollars, and I can send word to the old chap this very afternoon. It will make him happy for the rest of his life."

" No—no—no, not three dollars, nor three cents."

Miss Douglass made a gesture of despair. She might have expected that she could not move Lloyd. Once her mind was made up, one might argue with her till one's breath failed. She shook her head at Lloyd and exclaimed, but not ill-naturedly:

" Obstinate! Obstinate! Obstinate! "

Lloyd put away the hypodermic syringe and the minim-glass in their places in the bag, added a little ice-pick to its contents, and shut the bag with a snap.

" Now," she announced, " I'm ready."

When Miss Douglass had taken herself away Lloyd settled herself in the place she had vacated, and, stripping the wrappings from the books and magazines she had bought, began to turn the pages, looking at the pictures. But her interest flagged. She tried to read, but soon cast the book from her and leaned back upon the great couch, her hands clasped behind the great bronze-red coils at the back of her head, her dull-blue eyes fixed and vacant.

For hours the preceding night she had lain broad awake in her bed, staring at the shifting shadow pictures that the electric lights, shining through the trees down in the square, threw upon the walls and ceiling of her room. She had eaten but little since morning; a growing spirit of unrest had possessed her for the last two days. Now it had reached a head. She could no longer put her thoughts from her.

It had all come back again for the fiftieth time, for the hundredth time, the old, intolerable burden of anxiety growing heavier month by month, year by year. It seemed to her that a shape of terror, formless, intangible, and invisible, was always by her, now withdrawing, now advancing, but always there; there close at hand in some dark corner where she could not see, ready at every instant to assume a terrible and all too well-known form, and to jump at her from behind, from out the dark, and to clutch her throat with cold fingers. The thing played with her, tormented her; at times it all but disappeared; at times she believed she had fought it from her for good, and then she would wake of a night, in the stillness and in the dark, and know it to be there once more—at her bedside—at her back—at her throat—till her heart went wild with fear, and the suspense of waiting for an Enemy that would not strike, but that lurked and leered in dark corners, wrung from her a suppressed cry of anguish and exasperation, and drove her from her sleep with streaming eyes and tight-shut hands and wordless prayers.

For a few moments Lloyd lay back upon the couch, then regained her feet with a brusque, harassed movement of head and shoulders.

"Ah, no," she exclaimed under her breath, "it is too dreadful."

She tried to find diversion in her room, rearranging the few ornaments, winding the clock that struck ships' bells instead of hours, and turning the wicks of the old empire lamps that hung in brass brackets on either side the fireplace. Lloyd, after building the agency, had felt no scruple in choosing the best room in the house and furnishing it according to her taste. Her room was beautiful, but very simple in its appointments. There were great flat wall-spaces unspoiled by bric-à-brac, the floor marquetry, with but few rugs. The fireplace and its appurtenances were of brass. Her writing-desk, a huge affair, of ancient and almost black San Domingo mahogany.

But soon she wearied of the small business of pottering about her clock and lamps, and, turning to the window, opened it, and, leaning upon her elbows, looked down into the square.

By now the thunderstorm was gone, like the withdrawal of a dark curtain; the sun was out again over the City. The square, deserted but half an hour ago, was reinvaded with its little people of nurse-

maids, gray-coated policemen, and loungers reading
their papers on the benches near the fountain. The
elms still dripped, their wet leaves glistening again
to the sun. There was a delicious smell in the air—
a smell of warm, wet grass, of leaves and drenched
bark from the trees. On the far side of the square,
seen at intervals in the spaces between the foliage,
a passing truck painted vermilion set a brisk note
of colour in the scene. A newsboy appeared chanting the evening editions. On a sudden and from
somewhere close at hand an unseen hand-piano
broke out into a gay, jangling quickstep, marking
the time with delightful precision.

A carriage, its fine lacquered flanks gleaming in
the sunlight, rolled through the square, on its way,
no doubt, to the very fashionable quarter of the City
just beyond. Lloyd had a glimpse of the girl leaning back in its cushions, a girl of her own age, with
whom she had some slight acquaintance. For a
moment Lloyd, ridden with her terrors, asked herself if this girl, with no capabilities for either great
happiness or great sorrow, were not perhaps, after
all, happier than she. But she recoiled instantly,
murmuring to herself with a certain fierce energy:

" No, no; after all, I have lived."

And how had she lived? For the moment Lloyd
was willing to compare herself with the girl in the
landau. Swiftly she ran over her own life from the
time when left an orphan; in the year of her majority
she had become her own mistress and the mistress
of the Searight estate. But even at that time she
had long since broken away from the conventional
world she had known. Lloyd was a nurse in the

great St. Luke's Hospital even then, had been a probationer there at the time of her mother's death, six months before. She had always been ambitious, but vaguely so, having no determined object in view. She recalled how at that time she knew only that she was in love with her work, her chosen profession, and was accounted the best operating nurse in the ward.

She remembered, too, the various steps of her advancement, the positions she had occupied; probationer first, then full member of the active corps, next operating nurse, then ward manager, and, after her graduation, head nurse of ward four, where the maternity cases were treated. Then had come the time when she had left the hospital and practised private nursing by herself, and at last, not so long ago, the day when her Idea had so abruptly occurred to her; when her ambition, no longer vague, no longer personal, had crystallised and taken shape; when she had discovered a use for her money and had built and founded the house on Calumet Square. For a time she had been the superintendent of nurses here, until her own theories and ideas had obtained and prevailed in its management. Then, her work fairly started, she had resigned her position to an older woman, and had taken her place in the rank and file of the nurses themselves. She wished to be one of them, living the same life, subject to the same rigorous discipline, and to that end she had never allowed it to be known that she was the founder of the house. The other nurses knew that she was very rich, very independent and self-reliant, but that was all. Lloyd did not know and cared very little how they explained the origin and support of the agency.

Lloyd was animated by no great philanthropy, no vast love of humanity in her work; only she wanted, with all her soul she wanted, to count in the general economy of things; to choose a work and do it; to help on, *donner un coup d'epaule;* and this, supported by her own stubborn energy and her immense wealth, she felt that she was doing. To *do* things had become her creed; to do things, not to think them; to do things, not to talk them; to do things, not to read them. No matter how lofty the thoughts, how brilliant the talk, how beautiful the literature—for her, first, last, and always, were acts, acts, acts—concrete, substantial, material acts. The greatest and happiest day of her life had been when at last she laid her bare hand upon the rough, hard stone of the house in the square and looked up at the façade, her dull-blue eyes flashing with the light that so rarely came to them, while she murmured between her teeth:

" I—did—this."

As she recalled this moment now, leaning upon her elbows, looking down upon the trees and grass and asphalt of the square, and upon a receding landau, a wave of a certain natural pride in her strength, the satisfaction of attainment, came to her. Ah! she was better than other women; ah! she was stronger than other women; she was carrying out a splendid work. She straightened herself to her full height abruptly, stretching her outspread hands vaguely to the sunlight, to the City, to the world, to the great engine of life whose lever she could grasp and could control, smiling proudly, almost insolently, in the consciousness of her strength, the fine steadfastness of her purpose. Then all at once the smile was struck from her lips, the stiffness of her poise suddenly relaxed. There, there it was again, the terror, the dreadful fear she dared not name, back in its place once more—at her side, at her shoulder, at her throat, ready to clutch at her from out the dark.

She wheeled from the window, from the sunlight, her hands clasped before her trembling lips, the tears brimming her dull-blue eyes. For forty-eight hours she had fought this from her. But now it was no longer to be resisted.

" No, no," she cried half aloud. " I am no better, no stronger than the others. What does it all amount to when I know that, after all, I am just a woman—just a woman whose heart is slowly breaking? "

But there was an interruption. Rownie had knocked twice at her door before Lloyd had heard her. When Lloyd had opened the door the girl handed her a card with an address written on it in the superintendent's hand.

"This here jus' now come in f'om Dr. Street, Miss Lloyd," said Rownie; " Miss Bergyn " (this was the superintendent nurse) " ast me to give it to you."

It was a call to an address that seemed familiar to Lloyd at first; but she did not stop at that moment to reflect. Her stable telephone hung against the wall of the closet. She rang for Lewis, and while waiting for him to get around dressed for the street,

A Man's Woman

For the moment, at the prospect of action, even her haunting fear drew off and stood away from her. She was absorbed in her work upon the instant—alert, watchful, self-reliant. What the case was she could only surmise. How long she would be away she had no means of knowing—a week, a month, a year, she could not tell. But she was ready for any contingency. Usually the doctors informed the nurses as to the nature of the case at the time of sending for them, but Dr. Street had not done so now.

However, Rownie called up to her that her coupé was at the door. Lloyd caught up her satchels and ran down the stairs, crying good-bye to Miss Douglass, whom she saw at the farther end of the hall. In the hallway by the vestibule she changed the slide bearing her name from the top to the bottom of the roster.

"How about your mail?" cried Miss Douglass after her.

"Keep it here for me until I see how long I'm to be away," answered Lloyd, her hand upon the knob. "I'll let you know."

Lewis had put Rox in the shafts, and while the coupé spun over the asphalt at a smart clip Lloyd tried to remember where she had heard of the address before. Suddenly she snapped her fingers; she knew the case, had even been assigned to it some eight months before.

"Yes, yes, that's it—Campbell—wife dead—Lafayette Avenue—little daughter, Hattie—hip disease—hopeless—poor little baby."

Arriving at the house, Lloyd found the surgeon,

Dr. Street, and Mr. Campbell, who was a widower, waiting for her in a small drawing-room off the library. The surgeon was genuinely surprised and delighted to see her. Most of the doctors of the City knew Lloyd for the best trained nurse in the hospitals.

" Oh, it's you, Miss Searight; good enough! " The surgeon introduced her to the little patient's father, adding: " If any one can pull us through, Campbell, it will be Miss Searight."

The surgeon and nurse began to discuss the case.

" I think you know it already, don't you, Miss Searight? " said the surgeon. " You took care of it a while last winter. Well, there was a little improvement in the spring, not so much pain, but that in itself is a bad sign. We have done what we could, Farnham and I. But it don't yield to treatment; you know how these things are—stubborn. We made a preliminary examination yesterday. Sinuses have occurred, and the probe leads down to nothing but dead bone. Farnham and I had a consultation this morning. We must play our last card. I shall exsect the joint to-morrow."

Mr. Campbell drew in his breath and held it for a moment, looking out of the window.

Very attentive, Lloyd merely nodded her head, murmuring:

" I understand."

When Dr. Street had gone Lloyd immediately set to work. The operation was to take place at noon the following day, and she foresaw there would be no sleep for her that night. Street had left everything to her, even to the sterilising of his in-

struments. Until daylight the following morning
Lloyd came and went about the house with an untiring energy, yet with the silence of a swiftly moving shadow, getting together the things needed for
the operation—strychnia tablets, absorbent cotton,
the rubber tubing for the tourniquet, bandages, salt,
and the like—and preparing the little chamber adjoining the sick-room as an operating-room.

The little patient herself, Hattie, hardly into her
teens, remembered Lloyd at once. Before she went
to sleep Lloyd contrived to spend an hour in the sick-
room with her, told her as much as was necessary of
what was contemplated, and, by her cheery talk,
her gentleness and sympathy, inspired the little
girl with a certain sense of confidence and trust in
her.

" But—but—but just how bad will it hurt, Miss
Searight? " inquired Hattie, looking at her, wide-
eyed and serious.

" Dear, it won't hurt you at all; just two or three
breaths of the ether and you will be sound asleep.
When you wake up it will be all over and you will
be well."

Lloyd made the ether cone from a stiff towel, and
set it on Hattie's dressing-table. Last of all and
just before the operation the gauze sponges occupied her attention. The daytime brought her no
rest. Hattie was not to have any breakfast, but
toward the middle of the forenoon Lloyd gave her
a stimulating enema of whiskey and water, following it about an hour later by a hundredth grain of
atropia. She braided the little girl's hair in two
long plaits so that her head would rest squarely and

flatly upon the pillow. Hattie herself was now
ready for the surgeon.

Now there was nothing more to be done. Lloyd
could but wait. She took her place at the bedside
and tried to talk as lightly as was possible to her
patient. But now there was a pause in the round
of action. Her mind no longer keenly intent upon
the immediate necessities of the moment, began to
hark back again to the one great haunting fear that
for so long had overshadowed it. Even while she
exerted herself to be cheerful and watched for the
smiles on Hattie's face her hands twisted tight and
tighter under the folds of her blouse, and some
second self within her seemed to say:

"Suppose, suppose it should come, this thing I
dread but dare not name, what then, what then?
Should I not expect it? Is it not almost a certainty? Have I not been merely deceiving myself
with the forlornest hopes? Is it not the most
reasonable course to expect the worst? Do not all
indications point that way? Has not my whole life
been shaped to this end? Was not this calamity,
this mighty sorrow, prepared for me even before I
was born? And one can do nothing, absolutely
nothing, nothing, but wait and hope and fear, and
eat out one's heart with longing."

There was a knock at the door. Instead of calling to enter Lloyd went to it softly and opened it a
few inches. Mr. Campbell was there.

"They've come—Street and the assistant."

Lloyd heard a murmur of voices in the hall below
and the closing of the front door.

Farnham and Street went at once to the operating-room to make their hands and wrists aseptic. Campbell had gone downstairs to his smoking-room. It had been decided—though contrary to custom—that Lloyd should administer the chloroform.

At length Street tapped with the handle of a scalpel on the door to say that he was ready.

"Now, dear," said Lloyd, turning to Hattie, and picking up the ether cone.

But the little girl's courage suddenly failed her. She began to plead in a low voice choked with tears. Her supplications were pitiful; but Lloyd, once more intent upon her work, every faculty and thought concentrated upon what must be done, did not temporise an instant. Quietly she gathered Hattie's frail wrists in the grip of one strong palm, and held the cone to her face until she had passed off with a long sigh. She picked her up lightly, carried her into the next room, and laid her upon the operating-table. At the last moment Lloyd had busied herself with the preparation of her own person. Over her dress she passed her hospital blouse, which had been under a dry heat for hours. She rolled her sleeves up from her strong white forearms with their thick wrists and fine blue veining, and for upward of ten minutes scrubbed them with a new nail-brush in water as hot as she could bear it. After this she let her hands and forearms lie in the permanganate of potash solution till they were brown to the elbow, then washed away the stain in the oxalic-acid solution and in sterilised hot water. Street and Farnham, wearing their sterilised gowns and gloves, took their places. There was no conver-

sation. The only sounds were an occasional sigh
from the patient, a direction given in a low tone,
and, at intervals, the click of the knives and scalpel.
From outside the window came the persistent chirp-
ing of a band of sparrows.

Promptly the operation was begun; there was no
delay, no hesitation; what there was to be done had
been carefully planned beforehand, even to the mi-
nutest details. Street, a master of his profession,
thoroughly familiar with every difficulty that might
present itself during the course of the work in hand,
foreseeing every contingency, prepared for every
emergency, calm, watchful, self-contained, set about
the exsecting of the joint with no trace of compunction, no embarrassment, no misgiving. His assist-
ants, as well as he himself, knew that life or death
hung upon the issue of the next ten minutes. Upon
Street alone devolved the life of the little girl. A
second's hesitation at the wrong stage of the operation, a slip of bistoury or scalpel, a tremor of the
wrist, a single instant's clumsiness of the fingers,
and the Enemy—watching for every chance, intent
for every momentarily opened chink or cranny
wherein he could thrust his lean fingers—entered
the frail tenement with a leap, a rushing, headlong
spring that jarred the house of life to its foundations.
Lowering close over her head Lloyd felt the shadow
of his approach. He had arrived there in that commonplace little room, with its commonplace accessories, its ornaments, that suddenly seemed so trivial, so impertinent—the stopped French clock, with
its simpering, gilded cupids, on the mantelpiece; the
photograph of a number of picnickers " grouped "

on a hotel piazza gazing with monolithic cheerfulness at this grim business, this struggle of the two world forces, this crisis in a life.

Then abruptly the operation was over.

The nurse and surgeons eased their positions immediately, drawing long breaths. They began to talk, commenting upon the operation, and Lloyd, intensely interested, asked Street why he had, contrary to her expectations, removed the bone above the lesser trochanter. He smiled, delighted at her intelligence.

" It's better than cutting through the neck, Miss Searight," he told her. " If I had gone through the neck, don't you see, the trochanter major would come over the hole and prevent the discharges."

" Yes, yes, I see, of course," assented Lloyd.

The incision was sewn up, and when all was over Lloyd carried Hattie back to the bed in the next room. Slowly the little girl regained consciousness, and Lloyd began to regard her once more as a human being. During the operation she had forgotten the very existence of Hattie Campbell, a little girl she knew. She had only seen a bit of mechanism out of order and in the hands of a repairer. It was always so with Lloyd. Her charges were not infrequently persons whom she knew, often intimately, but during the time of their sickness their personalities vanished for the trained nurse; she saw only the " case," only the mechanism, only the deranged clockwork in imminent danger of running down.

But the danger was by no means over. The operation had been near the trunk. There had been considerable loss of blood, and the child's power of resistance had been weakened by long periods of suffering. Lloyd feared that the shock might prove too great. Farnham departed, but for a little while the surgeon remained with Lloyd to watch the symptoms. At length, however, he too, pressed for time, and expected at one of the larger hospitals of the City, went away, leaving directions for Lloyd to telephone him in case of the slightest change. At this hour, late in the afternoon, there were no indications that the little girl would not recover from the shock. Street believed she would rally and ultimately regain her health.

" But," he told Lloyd as he bade her good-bye, " I don't need to impress upon you the need of care and the greatest vigilance; absolute rest is the only thing; she must see nobody, not even her father. The whole system is numbed and deadened just yet, but there will be a change either for better or worse some time to-night."

For thirty-six hours Lloyd had not closed an eye, but of that she had no thought. Her supper was sent up to her, and she prepared herself for her night's watch. She gave the child such nourishment as she believed she could stand, and from time to time took her pulse, making records of it upon her chart for the surgeon's inspection later on. At intervals she took Hattie's temperature, placing the clinical thermometer in the armpit. Toward nine in the evening, while she was doing this for the third time within the hour, one of the house servants came to the room to inform her that she was wanted on the telephone. Lloyd hesitated, unwilling to leave

Hattie for an instant. However, the telephone was close at hand, and it was quite possible that Dr. Street had rung her up to ask for news.

But it was the agency that had called, and Miss Douglass informed her that a telegram had arrived there for her a few moments before. Should she hold it or send it to her by Rownie? Lloyd reflected a moment.

" Oh—open it and read it to me," she said. " It's a call, isn't it?—or—no; send it here by Rownie, and send my hospital slippers with her, the ones without heels. But don't ring up again to-night; we're expecting a crisis almost any moment."

Lloyd returned to the sick-room, sent away the servant, and once more settled herself for the night. Hattie had roused for a moment.

" Am I going to get well, am I going to get well, Miss Searight? "

Lloyd put her finger to her lips, nodding her head, and Hattie closed her eyes again with a long breath. A certain great tenderness and compassion for the little girl grew big in Lloyd's heart. To herself she said :

" God helping me, you shall get well. They believe in me, these people—' If any one could pull us through it would be Miss Searight.' We *will* ' pull through,' yes, for I'll do it."

The night closed down, dark and still and very hot. Lloyd, regulating the sick-room's ventilation, opened one of the windows from the top. The noises of the City steadily decreasing as the hours passed, reached her ears in a subdued, droning murmur. On her bed, that had for so long been her bed of pain, Hattie lay with closed eyes, inert, motionless, hardly seeming to breathe, her life in the balance; unhappy little invalid, wasted with suffering, with drawn, pinched face and bloodless lips, and at her side Lloyd, her dull-blue eyes never leaving her patient's face, alert and vigilant, despite her long wakefulness, her great bronze-red flame of hair rolling from her forehead and temples, the sombre glow in her cheeks no whit diminished by her day of fatigue, of responsibility and untiring activity.

For the time being she could thrust her fear, the relentless Enemy that for so long had hung upon her heels, back and away from her. There was another Enemy now to fight—or was it another—was it not the same Enemy, the very same, whose shadow loomed across that sickbed, across the frail, small body and pale, drawn face?

With her pity and compassion for the sick child there arose in Lloyd a certain unreasoned, intuitive obstinacy, a banding together of all her powers and faculties in one great effort at resistance, a steadfastness under great stress, a stubbornness, that shut its ears and eyes. It was her one dominant characteristic rising up, strong and insistent the instant she knew herself to be thwarted in her desires or checked in a course she believed to be right and good. And now as she felt the advance of the Enemy and saw the shadow growing darker across the bed her obstinacy hardened like tempered steel.

" No," she murmured, her brows levelled, her lips compressed, " she shall not die. I will not let her go."

A little later, perhaps an hour after midnight, at a

time when she believed Hattie to be asleep, Lloyd, watchful as ever, noted that her cheeks began alternately to puff out and contract with her breathing. In an instant the nurse was on her feet. She knew the meaning of this sign. Hattie had fainted while asleep. Lloyd took the temperature. It was falling rapidly. The pulse was weak, rapid, and irregular. It seemed impossible for Hattie to take a deep breath.

Then swiftly the expected crisis began to develop itself. Lloyd ordered Street to be sent for, but only as a matter of form. Long before he could arrive the issue would be decided. She knew that now Hattie's life depended on herself alone.

"Now," she murmured, as though the Enemy she fought could hear her, "now let us see who is the stronger. You or I."

Swiftly and gently she drew the bed from the wall and raised its foot, propping it in position with half a dozen books. Then, while waiting for the servants, whom she had despatched for hot blankets, administered a hypodermic injection of brandy.

"We will pull you through," she kept saying to herself, "we will pull you through. I shall not let you go."

The Enemy was close now, and the fight was hand to hand. Lloyd could almost feel, physically, actually, feel the slow, sullen, resistless pull that little by little was dragging Hattie's life from her grip. She set her teeth, holding back with all her might, bracing herself against the strain, refusing with all inborn stubbornness to yield her position.

"No—no," she repeated to herself, "you shall

not have her. I will not give her up; you shall not triumph over me."

Campbell was in the room, warned by the ominous coming and going of hushed footsteps.

"What is the use, nurse? It's all over. Let her die in peace. It's too cruel; let her die in peace."

The half-hour passed, then the hour. Once more Lloyd administered hypodermically the second dose of brandy. Campbell, unable to bear the sight, had withdrawn to the adjoining room, where he could be heard pacing the floor. From time to time he came back for a moment, whispering:

"Will she live, nurse? Will she live? Shall we pull her through?"

"I don't know," Lloyd told him. "I don't know. Wait. Go back. I will let you know."

Another fifteen minutes passed. Lloyd fancied that the heart's action was growing a little stronger. A great stillness had settled over the house. The two servants waiting Lloyd's orders in the hall outside the door refrained even from whispering. From the next room came the muffled sound of pacing footsteps, hurried, irregular, while with that strange perversity which seizes upon the senses at moments when they are more than usually acute Lloyd began to be aware of a vague, unwonted movement in the City itself, outside there behind the drawn curtains and half-opened window—a faint, uncertain agitation, a trouble, a passing ripple on the still black pool of the night, coming and going, and coming again, each time a little more insistent, each time claiming a little more attention and notice. It was about half past three o'clock. But the little patient's temperature was rising—there could be no doubt about that. The lungs expanded wider and deeper. Hattie's breathing was unmistakably easier; and as Lloyd put her fingers to the wrist she could hardly keep back a little exultant cry as she felt the pulse throbbing fuller, a little slower, a little more regularly. Now she redoubled her attention. Her hold upon the little life shut tighter; her power of resistance, her strength of purpose, seemed to be suddenly quadrupled. She could imagine the Enemy drawing off; she could think that the grip of cold fingers was loosening.

Slowly the crisis passed off, slowly the reaction began. Hattie was still unconscious, but there was a new look upon her face—a look that Lloyd had learned to know from long experience, an intangible and most illusive expression, nothing, something, the sign that only those who are trained to search for it may see and appreciate—the earliest faint flicker after the passing of the shadow.

" Will she live, will she live, nurse? " came Mr. Campbell's whisper at her shoulder.

" I think—I am almost sure—but we must not be too certain yet. Still there's a chance; yes, there's a chance."

Campbell, suddenly gone white, put out his hand and leaned a moment against the mantelpiece. He did not now leave the room. The door-bell rang.

" Dr. Street," murmured Lloyd.

But what had happened in the City? There in the still dark hours of that hot summer night an event of national, perhaps even international, importance had surely transpired. It was in the air—

a sense of a Great Thing come suddenly to a head somewhere in the world. Footsteps sounded rapidly on the echoing sidewalks. Here and there a street door opened. From corner to corner, growing swiftly nearer, came the cry of newsboys chanting extras. A subdued excitement was abroad, finding expression in a vague murmur, the mingling of many sounds into one huge note—a note that gradually swelled and grew louder and seemed to be rising from all corners of the City at once.

There was a step at the sick-room door. Dr. Street? No, Rownie—Rownie with two telegrams for Lloyd.

Lloyd took them from her, then with a sharp, brusque movement of her head and suddenly smitten with an idea, turned from them to listen to the low, swelling murmur of the City. These despatches—no, they were no " call " for her. She guessed what they might be. Why had they come to her now? Why was there this sense of some great tidings in the wind? The same tidings that had come to the world might come to her—in these despatches. Might it not be so? She caught her breath quickly. The terror, the fearful anxiety that had haunted and oppressed her for so long, was it to be lifted now at last? The Enemy that lurked in the dark corners, ever ready to clutch her, was it to be driven back and away from her forever? She dared not hope for it. But something was coming to her; she knew it, she felt it; something was preparing for her, coming to her swifter with every second—coming, coming, coming from out the north. She saw Dr. Street in the room, though how and when he had arrived she could not afterward recall. Her mind was all alert, intent upon other things, listening, waiting. The surgeon had been leaning over the bed. Suddenly he straightened up, saying aloud to Campbell:

"Good, good, we're safe. We have pulled through."

Lloyd tore open her telegrams. One was signed "Bennett," the other "Ferriss."

"Thank God!" exclaimed Mr. Campbell.

"Oh," cried Lloyd, a great sob shaking her from head to heel, a smile of infinite happiness flashing from her face. "Oh—yes, thank God, we—we *have* pulled through."

"Am I going to get well, am I going to get well, Miss Searight?" Hattie, once more conscious, raised her voice weak and faint.

Lloyd was on her knees beside her, her head bent over her.

"Hush; yes, dear, you are safe." Then the royal bronze-red hair bent lower still. The dull-blue eyes were streaming now, the voice one low quiver of sobs. Tenderly, gently Lloyd put an arm about the child, her head bending lower and lower. Her cheek touched Hattie's. For a moment the little girl, frail, worn, pitifully wasted, and the strong, vigorous woman, with her imperious will and indomitable purpose, rested their heads upon the same pillow, both broken with suffering, the one of the body, the other of the mind.

"Safe; yes, dear, safe," whispered Lloyd, her face all but hidden. "Safe, safe, and saved to me. Oh, dearest of all the world!"

A Man's Woman

And then to her ears the murmur of the City seemed to leap suddenly to articulate words, the clanging thunder of the entire nation—the whole round world thrilling with this great news that had come to it from out the north in the small hours of this hot summer's night. And the chanting cries of the street rolled to her like the tremendous diapason of a gigantic organ:

"Rescued, rescued, rescued!"

IV.

On the day that Lloyd returned to the house on Calumet Square (Hattie's recovery being long since assured), and while she was unpacking her valise and settling herself again in her room, a messenger boy brought her a note.

Have just arrived in the City. When may I see you?
                                                    BENNETT.

News of Ward Bennett and of Richard Ferriss had not been wanting during the past fortnight or so. Their names and that of the ship herself, even the names of Adler, Hansen, Clarke, and Dennison, even Muck Tu, even that of Kamiska, the one surviving dog, filled the mouths and minds of men to the exclusion of everything else.

The return of the expedition after its long imprisonment in the ice and at a time when all hope of its safety had been abandoned was one of the great events of that year. The fact that the expedition had failed to reach the Pole, or to attain any unusual high latitude, was forgotten or ignored. Nothing was remembered but the masterly retreat toward Kolyuchin Bay, the wonderful march over the ice, the indomitable courage, unshaken by hardship, perils, obstacles, and privations almost beyond imagination. All this, together with a multitude of details, some of them palpably fictitious, the press of the City where Bennett and Ferriss both had their homes published and republished and published again and again. News of the men, their whereabouts and intentions, invaded the sick-room —where Lloyd watched over the convalescence of her little patient—by the very chinks of the windows.

Lloyd learned how the ship had been "nipped;" how, after inconceivable toil, the members of the expedition had gained the land; how they had marched southward toward the Chuckch settlements; how, at the eleventh hour, the survivors, exhausted and starving, had been rescued by the steam whalers; how these whalers themselves had been caught in the ice, and how the survivors of the Freja had been obliged to spend another winter in the Arctic. She learned the details of their final return. In the quiet, darkened room where Hattie lay she heard from without the echo of the thunder of the nations; she saw how the figure of Bennett towered suddenly magnificent in the world; how that the people were brusquely made aware of a new hero. She learned that honours came thronging about him unsought; that the King of the Belgians had conferred a decoration upon him; that the geographical societies of continental Europe had elected him to honourary membership; that the President and the Secretary of War had sent telegrams of congratulations.

"And what does he do," she murmured, "the first of all upon his return? Asks to see me—me!"

She sent an answer to his note by the same boy

who brought it, naming the following afternoon, explaining that two days later she expected to go into the country to a little town called Bannister to take her annual fortnight's vacation.

" But what of—of the other? " she murmured as she stood at the window of her room watching the messenger boy bicycling across the square. " Why does not he—he, too——? "

She put her chin in the air and turned about, looking abstractedly at the rugs on the parquetry.

Lloyd's vacation had really begun two days before. Her name was off the roster of the house, and till the end of the month her time was her own. The afternoon was hot and very still. Even in the cool, stone-built agency, with its windows wide and heavily shaded with awnings, the heat was oppressive. For a long time Lloyd had been shut away from fresh air and the sun, and now she suddenly decided to drive out in the City's park. She rang up her stable and ordered Lewis to put her ponies to her phaëton.

She spent a delightful two hours in the great park, losing herself in its farthest, shadiest, and most unfrequented corners. She drove herself, and intelligently. Horses were her passion, and not Lewis himself understood their care and management better. Toward the cool of the day and just as she had pulled the ponies down to a walk in a long, deserted avenue overspanned with elms and great cottonwoods she was all at once aware of an open carriage that had turned into the far end of the same avenue approaching at an easy trot. It drew near, and she saw that its only occupant was a man leaning back rather limply in the cushions. As the eye of the trained nurse fell upon him she at once placed him in the category of convalescents or chronic invalids, and she was vaguely speculating as to the nature of his complaint when the carriage drew opposite her phaëton, and she recognised Richard Ferriss.

Ferriss, but not the same Ferriss to whom she had said good-bye on that never-to-be-forgotten March afternoon, with its gusts and rain, four long years ago. The Ferriss she had known then had been an alert, keen man, with quick, bright eyes, alive to every impression, responsive to every sensation, living his full allowance of life. She was looking now at a man unnaturally old, of deadened nerves, listless. As he caught sight of her and recognised her he suddenly roused himself with a quick, glad smile and with a look in his eyes that to Lloyd was unmistakable. But there was not that joyful, exuberant start she had anticipated, and, for that matter, wished. Neither did Lloyd set any too great store by the small amenities of life, but that Ferriss should remain covered hurt her a little. She wondered how she could note so trivial a detail at such a moment. But this was Ferriss.

Her heart was beating fast and thick as she halted her ponies. The driver of the carriage jumped down and held the door for Ferriss, and the chief engineer stepped quickly toward her.

So it was they met after four years—and such years—unexpectedly, without warning or preparation, and not at all as she had expected. What they said to each other in those first few moments Lloyd could never afterward clearly remember. One incident alone detached itself vividly from the blur.

"I have just come from the square," Ferriss had explained, "and they told me that you had left for a drive out here only the moment before, so there was nothing for it but to come after you."

"Shan't we walk a little?" she remembered she had asked after a while. "We can have the carriages wait; or do you feel strong enough? I forgot——"

But he interrupted her, protesting his fitness.

"The doctor merely sent me out to get the air, and it's humiliating to be wheeled about like an old woman."

Lloyd passed the reins back of her to Lewis, and, gathering her skirts about her, started to descend from the phaëton. The step was rather high from the ground. Ferriss stood close by. Why did he not help her? Why did he stand there, his hands in his pockets, so listless and unconscious of her difficulty. A little glow of irritation deepened the dull crimson of her cheeks. Even returned Arctic explorers could not afford to ignore entirely life's little courtesies—and he of all men.

"Well," she said, expectantly hesitating before attempting to descend.

Then she caught Ferriss's eyes fixed upon her. He was smiling a little, but the dull, stupefied expression of his face seemed for a brief instant to give place to one of great sadness. He raised a shoulder resignedly, and Lloyd, with the suddenness of a blow, remembered that Ferriss had no hands.

She dropped back in the seat of the phaëton, covering her eyes, shaken and unnerved for the moment with a great thrill of infinite pity—of shame at her own awkwardness, and of horror as for one brief instant the smiling summer park, the afternoon's warmth, the avenue of green, over-arching trees, the trim, lacquered vehicles and glossy-brown horses were struck from her mind, and she had a swift vision of the Ice, the darkness of the winter night, the lacerating, merciless cold, the blinding, whirling, dust-like snow.

For half an hour they walked slowly about in the park, the carriages following at a distance. They did not talk very much. It seemed to Lloyd that she would never tire of scrutinising his face, that her interest in his point of view, his opinions, would never flag. He had had an experience that came but to few men. For four years he had been out of the world, had undergone privation beyond conception. What now was to be his attitude? How had he changed? That he had not changed to her Lloyd knew in an instant. He still loved her; that was beyond all doubt. But this terrible apathy that seemed now to be a part of him! She had heard of the numbing stupor that invades those who stay beyond their time in the Ice, but never before had she seen it in its reality. It was not a lack of intelligence; it seemed rather to be the machinery of intelligence rusted and clogged from long disuse. He deliberated long before he spoke. It took him some time to understand things. Speech did not come to him readily, and he became easily confused in the matter of words. Once, suddenly, he had interrupted her, breaking out with:

A Man's Woman

"Oh, the smell of the trees, of the grass! Isn't it wonderful; isn't it wonderful?" And a few seconds later, quite irrelevantly: "And, after all, we failed."

At once Lloyd was all aroused, defending him against himself.

"Failed! And you say that? If you did not reach the Pole, what then? The world will judge you by results perhaps, and the world's judgment will be wrong. Is it nothing that you have given the world an example of heroism——"

"Oh, don't call it that."

"Of heroism, of courage, of endurance? Is it nothing that you have overcome obstacles before which other men would have died? Is it nothing that you have shown us all how to be patient, how to be strong? There are some things better even than reaching the Pole. To suffer and be calm is one of them; not to give up—never to be beaten—is another. Oh, if I were a man! Ten thousand, a hundred thousand people are reading to-night of what you have done—of what you have done, you understand, not of what you have failed to do. They have seen—you have shown them what the man can do who says *I will,* and you have done a little more, have gone a little further, have been a little braver, a little hardier, a little nobler, a little more determined than any one has ever been before. Whoever fails now cannot excuse himself by saying that he has done as much as a man can do. He will have to remember the men of the Freja. He will have to remember you. Don't you suppose I am proud of you; don't you suppose that I am stronger and

6   81

better because of what you have done? Do you
think it is nothing for me to be sitting here beside
you, here in this park—to be—yes, to be with you?
Can't you understand? Isn't it something to me
that you are the man you are; not the man whose
name the people are shouting just now, not the man
to whom a king gave a bit of ribbon and enamel,
but the man who lived like a man, who would not
die just because it was easier to die than to live,
who fought like a man, not only for himself but for
the lives of those he led, who showed us all how to be
strong, and how strong one could be if one would
only try? What does the Pole amount to? The
world wants men, great, strong, harsh, brutal men—
men with purposes, who let nothing, nothing, nothing stand in their way."

"You mean Bennett," said Ferriss, looking up
quickly. "You commenced by speaking of me,
but it's Bennett you are talking of now."

But he caught her glance and saw that she was
looking steadfastly at him—at him. A look was in
her face, a light in her dull-blue eyes, that he had
never seen there before.

"Lloyd," he said quietly, "which one of us, Bennett or I, were you speaking of just then? You
know what I mean; which one of us?"

"I was speaking of the man who was strong
enough to do great things," she said.

Ferriss drew the stumps of his arms from his
pockets and smiled at them grimly.

"H'm, can one do much—this way?" he muttered.

With a movement she did not try to restrain

Lloyd put both her hands over his poor, shapeless wrists. Never in her life had she been so strongly moved. Pity, such as she had never known, a tenderness and compassion such as she had never experienced, went knocking at her breast. She had no words at hand for so great emotions. She longed to tell him what was in her heart, but all speech failed.

"Don't!" she exclaimed. "Don't! I will not have you."

A little later, as they were returning toward the carriages, Lloyd, after a moment's deliberation upon the matter, said:

"Can't I set you down somewhere near your rooms? Let your carriage go."

He shook his head: "I've just given up my downtown rooms. Bennett and I have taken other rooms much farther uptown. In fact, I believe I am supposed to be going there now. It would be quite out of your way to take me there. We are much quieter out there, and people can't get at us so readily. The doctor says we both need rest after our shaking up. Bennett himself—iron as he is—is none too strong, and what with the mail, the telegrams, reporters, deputations, editors, and visitors, and the like, we are kept on something of a strain. Besides we have still a good deal of work to do getting our notes into shape."

Lewis brought the ponies to the edge of the walk, and Lloyd and Ferriss separated, she turning the ponies' heads homeward, starting away at a brisk trot, and leaving him in his carriage, which he had directed to carry him to his new quarters.

A Man's Woman

But at the turn of the avenue Lloyd leaned from the phaëton and looked back. The carriage was just disappearing down the vista of elms and cottonwoods. She waved her hand gayly, and Ferriss responded with the stump of one forearm.

On the next day but one, a Friday, Lloyd was to go to the country. Every year in the heat of the summer Lloyd spent her short vacation in the sleepy and old-fashioned little village of Bannister. The country around the village was part of the Searight estate. It was quiet, off the railroad, just the place to forget duties, responsibilities, and the wearing anxieties of sick-rooms. But Thursday afternoon she expected Bennett.

Thursday morning she was in her room. Her trunk was already packed. There was nothing more to be done. She was off duty. There was neither care nor responsibility upon her mind. But she was too joyful, too happily exalted, too exuberant in gayety to pass her time in reading. She wanted action, movement, life, and instinctively threw open a window of her room, and, according to her habit, leaned upon her elbows and looked out and down upon the square. The morning was charming. Later in the day it probably would be very hot, but as yet the breeze of the earliest hours was stirring nimbly. The cool of it put a brisker note in the sombre glow of her cheeks, and just stirred a lock that, escaping from her gorgeous coils of dark-red hair, hung curling over her ear and neck. Into her eyes of dull blue—like the blue of old china—the morning's sun sent an occasional unwonted sparkle. Over the asphalt and over the green grass-plots of the square the shadows of the venerable elms wove a shifting maze of tracery. Traffic avoided the place. It was invariably quiet in the square, and one—as now—could always hear the subdued ripple and murmur of the fountain in the centre.

But the crowning delight of that morning was the sudden appearance of a robin in a tree close to Lloyd's window. He was searching his breakfast. At every moment he came and went between the tree-tops and the grass-plots, very important, very preoccupied, chittering and calling the while, as though he would never tire. Lloyd whistled to him, and instantly he answered, cocking his head sideways. She whistled again, and he piped back an impudent response, and for quite five minutes the two held an elaborate altercation between tree-top and window-ledge. Lloyd caught herself laughing outright and aloud for no assignable reason. " Ah, the world was a pretty good place after all ! "

A little later, and while she was still at the window, Rownie brought her a note from Bennett, sent by special messenger.

Ferriss woke up sick this morning. Nobody here but the two of us; can't leave him alone.   BENNETT.

" Oh! " exclaimed Lloyd Searight a little blankly.

The robin and his effrontery at once ceased to be amusing. She closed the window abruptly, shutting out the summer morning's gayety and charm, turning her back upon the sunlight.

Now she was more in the humour of reading. On the great divan against the wall lay the month's

magazines and two illustrated weeklies. Lloyd had
bought them to read on the train. But now she
settled herself upon the divan and, picking up one
of the weeklies, turned its leaves listlessly. All at
once she came upon two pictures admirably reproduced from photographs, and serving as illustra-
tions to the weekly's main article—" The Two
Leaders of the Freja Expedition." One was a picture of Bennett, the other of Ferriss.

The suddenness with which she had come upon
his likeness almost took Lloyd's breath from her.
It was the last thing she had expected. If he himself had abruptly entered the room in person she
could hardly have been more surprised. Her heart
gave a great leap, the dull crimson of her cheeks
shot to her forehead. Then, with a charming movement, at once impulsive and shamefaced, smiling
the while, her eyes half-closing, she laid her cheek
upon the picture, murmuring to herself words that
only herself should hear. The next day she left
for the country.

On that same day when Dr. Pitts arrived at the
rooms Ferriss and Bennett had taken he found the
anteroom already crowded with visitors—a knot of
interviewers, the manager of a lecture bureau, as
well as the agent of a patented cereal (who sought
the man of the hour for an endorsement of his article), and two female reporters.

Decidedly Richard Ferriss was ill; there could
be no doubt about that. Bennett had not slept the
night before, but had gone to and fro about the
rooms tending to his wants with a solicitude and a
gentleness that in a man so harsh and so toughly

fibred seemed strangely out of place. Bennett was
far from well himself. The terrible milling which
he had undergone had told even upon that enormous frame, but his own ailments were promptly
ignored now that Ferriss, the man of all men to him,
was " down."

"I didn't pull through with you, old man," he
responded to all of Ferriss's protests, " to have you
get sick on my hands at this time of day. No more
of your damned foolishness now. Here's the quinine. Down with it!"

Bennett met Pitts at the door of Ferriss's room,
and before going in drew him into a corner.

"He's a sick boy, Pitts, and is going to be worse,
though he's just enough of a fool boy not to admit
it. I've seen them start off this gait before. Remember, too, when you look him over that it's not
as though he had been in a healthy condition before.
Our work in the ice ground him down about as fine
as he could go and yet live, and the hardtack and
salt pork on the steam whalers were not a good
diet for a convalescent. And see here, Pitts," said
Bennett, clearing his throat, " I—well, I'm rather
fond of that fool boy in there. We are not taking
any chances, you understand."

After the doctor had seen the chief engineer and
had prescribed calomel and a milk diet, Bennett followed him out into the hall and accompanied him
to the door.

"Verdict?" he demanded, fixing the physician
intently with his small, distorted eyes. But Pitts
was non-committal.

"Yes, he's a sick boy, but the thing, whatever it

is going to be, has been gathering slowly. He complains of headache, great weakness and nausea, and you speak of frequent nose-bleeds during the night. The abdomen is tender upon pressure, which is a symptom I would rather not have found. But I can't make any positive diagnosis as yet. Some big sickness is coming on—that, I am afraid, is certain. I shall come out here to-morrow. But, Mr. Bennett, be careful of yourself. Even stee' can weaken, you know. You see this rabble " (he motioned with his head toward the anteroom, where the other visitors were waiting) " that is hounding you? Everybody knows where you are. Man, you must have rest. I don't need to look at you more than once to know that. Get away! Get away even from your mails! Hide from everybody for a while! Don't think you can nurse your friend through these next few weeks, because you can't."

"Well," answered Bennett, "wait a few days. We'll see by the end of the week."

The week passed. Ferriss went gradually from bad to worse, though as yet the disease persistently refused to declare itself. He was quite helpless, and Bennett watched over him night and day, pottering around him by the hour, giving him his medicines, cooking his food, and even when Ferriss complained of the hotness of the bedclothes, changing the very linen that he might lie upon cool sheets. But at the end of the week Dr. Pitts declared that Bennett himself was in great danger of breaking down, and was of no great service to the sick man.

"To-morrow," said the doctor, " I shall have a young fellow here who happens to be a cousin of mine. He is an excellent trained nurse, a fellow we can rely upon. He'll take your place. I'll have him here to-morrow, and you must get away. Hide somewhere. Don't even allow your mail to be forwarded. The nurse and I will take care of Mr. Ferriss. You can leave me your address, and I will wire you if it is necessary. Now be persuaded like a reasonable man. I will stake my professional reputation that you will knock under if you stay here with a sick man on your hands and newspaper men taking the house by storm at all hours of the day. Come now, will you go? Mr. Ferriss is in no danger, and you will do him more harm by staying than by going. So long as you remain here you will have this raft of people in the rooms at all hours. Deny yourself! Keep them out! Keep out the American reporter when he goes gunning for a returned explorer! Do you think this," and he pointed again to the crowd in the anteroom, " is the right condition for a sick man's quarters? You are imperilling his safety, to say nothing of your own, by staying beside him—you draw the fire, Mr. Bennett."

" Well, there's something in that," muttered Bennett, pulling at his mustache. " But—" Bennett hesitated, then: " Pitts, I want you to take my place here if I go away. Have a nurse if you like, but I shouldn't feel justified in leaving the boy in his condition unless I knew you were with him continually. I don't know what your practice is worth to you, say for a month, or until the boy is out of danger, but make me a proposition. I think we can come to an understanding."

" But it won't be necessary to have a doctor with Mr. Ferriss constantly. I should see him every day and the nurse——"

Bennett promptly overrode his objections. Harshly and abruptly he exclaimed: " I'm not taking any chances. It shall be as I say. I want the boy well, and I want you and the nurse to see to it that he *gets* well. I'll meet the expenses."

Bennett did not hear the doctor's response and his suggestion as to the advisability of taking Ferriss to his own house in the country while he could be moved. For the moment he was not listening. An idea had abruptly presented itself to him. He was to go to the country. But where? A grim smile began to relax the close-gripped lips and the hard set of the protruding jaw. He tugged again at his mustache, scowling at the doctor, trying to hide his humour.

" Well, that's settled then," he said; " I'll get away to-morrow—somewhere."

" Whereabouts? " demanded the doctor. " I shall want to let you know how we progress."

Bennett chose to feel a certain irritation. What business of Pitts was it whom he went to see, or, rather, where he meant to go?

" You told me to hide away from everybody, not even to allow my mail to be forwarded. But I'll let you know where to reach me, of course, as soon as I get there. It won't be far from town."

" And I will take your place here with Mr. Ferriss; somebody will be with him at every moment, and I shall only wire you," continued the doctor, " in case of urgent necessity. I want you to have all the rest you can, and stay away as long as possible. I shan't annoy you with telegrams unless I must. You'll understand that no news is good news."

On that particular morning Lloyd sat in her room in the old farmhouse that she always elected to call her home as often as she visited Bannister. It was some quarter of a mile outside the little village, and on the road that connected it with the railway at Fourth Lake, some six miles over the hills to the east. It was yet early in the morning, and Lloyd was writing letters that she would post at Fourth Lake later in the forenoon. She intended driving over to the lake. Two days before, Lewis had arrived with Rox, the ponies and the phaëton. Lloyd's dog-cart, a very gorgeous, high-wheeled affair, was always kept at Bannister.

The room in which she now sat was delightful. Everything was white, from the curtains of the bed to the chintz hangings on the walls. A rug of white fur was on the floor. The panellings and wooden shutters of the windows were painted white. The fireplace was set in glossy-white tiles, and its opening covered with a screen of white feathers. The windows were flung wide, and a great flood of white sunlight came pouring into the room. Lloyd herself was dressed in white, from the clean, crisp scarf tied about her neck to the tip of her canvas tennis shoes. And in all this array of white only the dull-red flame of her high-piled hair—in the sunshine glowing like burnished copper—set a vivid note of colour, the little strands and locks about her neck and ears coruscating as the breeze from the open windows stirred them.

The morning was veritably royal—still, cool, and odorous of woods and cattle and growing grass. A great sense of gayety, of exhilaration, was in the air. Lloyd was all in tune with it. While she wrote her left elbow rested on the table, and in her left hand she held a huge, green apple, unripe, sour, delicious beyond words, and into which she bit from time to time with the silent enjoyment of a schoolgirl.

Her letter was to Hattie's father, Mr. Campbell, and she wrote to ask if the little girl might not spend a week with her at Bannister. When the letter was finished and addressed she thrust it into her belt, and, putting on her hat, ran downstairs. Lewis had brought the dog-cart to the gate, and stood waiting in the road by Rox's head. But as Lloyd went down the brick-paved walk of the front yard Mrs. Applegate, who owned the farmhouse, and who was at once Lloyd's tenant, landlady, housekeeper, and cook, appeared on the porch of the house, the head of a fish in her hand, and Charley-Joe, the yellow tomcat, at her heels, eyeing her with painful intentness.

"Say, Miss Searight," she called, her forearm across her forehead to shade her eyes, the hand still holding the fish's head, " say, while you're out this morning will you keep an eye out for that dog of our'n—you know, Dan—the one with liver'n white spots? He's run off again—ain't seen him since yesterday noon. He gets away an' goes off fighting other dogs over the whole blessed county. There ain't a dog big 'r little within ten mile that

Dan ain't licked. He'd sooner fight than he would
eat, that dog."

"I will, I will," answered Lloyd, climbing to the
high seat, "and if I find him I shall drag him back
by the scruff of his neck. Good-morning, Lewis.
Why have you put the overhead check on Rox?"

Lewis touched his cap.

"He feels his oats some this morning, and if he
gets his lower jaw agin' his chest there's no holding of him, Miss—no holding of him in the world."

Lloyd gathered up the reins and spoke to the
horse, and Lewis stood aside.

Rox promptly went up into the air on his hind
legs, shaking his head with a great snort.

"Steady, you old pig," said Lloyd, calmly. "Soh,
soh, who's trying to kill you?"

"Hadn't I better come with you, Miss?" inquired Lewis anxiously.

Lloyd shook her head. "No, indeed," she said
decisively.

Rox, after vindicating his own independence by
the proper amount of showing off, started away
down the road with as high an action as he could
command, playing to the gallery, looking back and
out of the tail of his eye to see if Lewis observed
what a terrible fellow he was that morning.

"Well, of all the critters!" commented Mrs.
Applegate from the porch. But Charley-Joe, with
an almost hypnotic fixity in his yellow eyes, and
who during the last few minutes had several times
opened his mouth wide in an ineffectual attempt to
mew, suddenly found his voice with a prolonged
and complaining note.

"Well, heavens an' airth, take your fish, then!"
exclaimed Mrs. Applegate suddenly, remembering
the cat. "An' get off'n my porch with it." She
pushed him away with the side of her foot, and
Charley-Joe, with the fish's head in his teeth, retired
around the corner of the house by the rain barrel,
where at intervals he could be heard growling to
himself in a high-pitched key, pretending the approach of some terrible enemy.

Meanwhile Lloyd, already well on her way, was
having an exciting tussle with Rox. The horse had
begun by making an exhibition of himself for all
who could see, but in the end he had so worked upon
his own nerves that instead of frightening others
he only succeeded in terrifying himself. He was
city-bred, and the sudden change from brick houses
to open fields had demoralised him. He began to
have a dim consciousness of just how strong he was.
There was nothing vicious about him. He would
not have lowered himself to kick, but he did want,
with all the big, strong heart of him, to run.

But back of him there—he felt it thrilling along
the tense-drawn reins—was a calm, powerful grip,
even, steady, masterful. Turn his head he could
not, but he knew very well that Lloyd had taken a
double twist upon the reins, and that her hands, even
if they were gloved in white, were strong—strong
enough to hold him to his work. And besides this
—he could tell it by the very feel of the bit—he knew
that she did not take him very seriously, that he
could not make her afraid of him. He knew that
she could tell at once whether he shied because he
was really frightened or because he wanted to break

the shaft, and that in the latter case he would get
the whip—and mercilessly, too—across his haunch,
a degradation, above all things, to be avoided. And
she had called him an old pig once already that
morning.

Lloyd drove on. She keenly enjoyed this struggle
between the horse's strength and her own determination, her own obstinacy. No, she would not
let Rox have his way; she would not allow him to
triumph over her for a single moment. She would
neither be forced nor tricked into yielding a single
point however small. She would be mistress of the
situation.

By the end of half an hour she had him well in
hand, and was bowling smoothly along a level stretch
of road at the foot of an abrupt rise of land covered
with scrub oak and broken with outcroppings of
granite of a curious formation. Just beyond here
the road crossed the canal by a narrow—in fact, a
much too narrow—plank bridge without guard-
rails. The wide-axled dog-cart had just sufficient
room on either hand, and Lloyd, too good a whip
to take chances with so nervous a horse as Rox,
drew him down to a walk as she approached it. But
of a sudden her eyes were arrested by a curious
sight. She halted the cart.

At the roadside, some fifty yards from the plank
bridge, were two dogs. Evidently there had just
been a dreadful fight. Here and there a stone was
streaked with blood. The grass and smaller bushes
were flattened out, and tufts of hair were scattered
about upon the ground. Of the two dogs, Lloyd
recognised one upon the instant. It was Dan, the

"liver'n white" fox-hound of the farmhouse—the fighter and terror of the country. But he was lying upon his side now, the foreleg broken, or rather crushed, as if in a vise; the throat torn open, the life-blood in a great pool about his head   He was dead, or in the very throes of death. Poor Dan, he had fought his last fight, had found more than his match at last.

Lloyd looked at the other dog—the victor; then looked at him a second time and a third.

"Well," she murmured, "that's a strange-looking dog."

In fact, he was a curious animal. His broad, strong body was covered with a brown fur as dense, as thick, and as soft as a wolf's; the ears were pricked and pointed, the muzzle sharp, the eyes slant and beady. The breast was disproportionately broad, the forelegs short and apparently very powerful. Around his neck was a broad nickelled collar.

But as Lloyd sat in the cart watching him he promptly demonstrated the fact that his nature was as extraordinary as his looks. He turned again from a momentary inspection of the intruders, sniffed once or twice at his dead enemy, then suddenly began to eat him.

Lloyd's gorge rose with anger and disgust. Even if Dan had been killed, it had been in fair fight, and there could be no doubt that Dan himself had been the aggressor. She could even feel a little respect for the conqueror of the champion, but to turn upon the dead foe, now that the heat of battle was past, and (in no spirit of hate or rage) deliberately to eat him. What a horror! She took out her whip.

A Man's Woman

" Shame on you!" she exclaimed. " Ugh! what
a savage; I shan't allow you!"

A farm-hand was coming across the plank bridge,
and as he drew near the cart Lloyd asked him to
hold Rox for a moment. Rox was one of those
horses who, when standing still, are docile as a
kitten, and she had no hesitancy in leaving him with
a man at his head. She jumped out, the whip in her
hand. Dan was beyond all help, but she wanted at
least to take his collar back to Mrs. Applegate. The
strange dog permitted himself to be driven off a
little distance. Part of his strangeness seemed to
be that through it all he retained a certain placidity
of temper. There was no ferocity in his desire to
eat Dan.

" That's just what makes it so disgusting," said
Lloyd, shaking her whip at him. He sat down upon
his haunches, eyeing her calmly, his tongue lolling. When she had unbuckled Dan's collar and
tossed it into the cart under the seat she inquired
of the farm-hand as to where the new dog came
from.

" It beats me, Miss Searight," he answered;
" never saw such a bird in these parts before; t'other
belongs down to Applegate's."

" Come, let's have a look at you," said Lloyd, putting back the whip; " let me see your collar."

Disregarding the man's warning, she went up to
the stranger, whistling and holding out her hand,
and he came up to her—a little suspiciously at first,
but in the end wagging his tail, willing to be
friendly. Lloyd parted the thick fur around his
neck and turned the plate of the collar to the light.

On the plate was engraved: " Kamiska, Arctic S. S. ' Freja.' Return to Ward Bennett."

" Anything on the collar? " asked the man.

Lloyd settled a hairpin in a coil of hair at the back of her neck.

" Nothing—nothing that I can make out."

She climbed into the cart again and dismissed the farm-hand with a quarter. He disappeared around the turn of the road. But as she was about to drive on, Lloyd heard a great clattering of stones upon the hill above her, a crashing in the bushes, and a shrill whistle thrice repeated. Kamiska started up at once, cocking alternate ears, then turned about and ran up the hill to meet Ward Bennett, who came scrambling down, jumping from one granite outcrop to another, holding on the whiles by the lower branches of the scrub oak-trees.

He was dressed as if for an outing, in knicker-bockers and huge, hob-nailed shoes. He wore an old shooting-coat and a woollen cap; a little leather sack was slung from his shoulder, and in his hand he carried a short-handled geologist's hammer.

And then, after so long a time, Lloyd saw his face again—the rugged, unhandsome face; the massive jaw, huge almost to deformity; the great, brutal, indomitable lips; the square-cut chin with its forward, aggressive thrust; the narrow forehead, seamed and contracted, and the twinkling, keen eyes so marred by the cast, so heavily shadowed by the shaggy eyebrows. When he spoke the voice came heavy and vibrant from the great chest, a harsh, deep bass, a voice in which to command men, not a voice in which to talk to women.

A Man's Woman

Lloyd, long schooled to self-repression and the control of her emotions when such repression and control were necessary, sat absolutely moveless on her high seat, her hands only shutting tighter and tighter upon the reins. She had often wondered how she would feel, what was to be her dominant impulse, at such moments as these, and now she realised that it was not so much joy, not so much excitement, as a resolute determination not for one instant to lose her poise.

She was thinking rapidly. For four years they had not met. At one time she believed him to be dead. But in the end he had been saved, had come back, and, ignoring the plaudits of an entire Christendom, had addressed himself straight to her. For one of them, at least, this meeting was a crisis. What would they first say to each other? how be equal to the situation? how rise to its dramatic possibilities? But the moment had come to them suddenly, had found them all unprepared. There was no time to think of adequate words. Afterward, when she reviewed this encounter, she told herself that they both had failed, and that if the meeting had been faithfully reproduced upon the stage or in the pages of a novel it would have seemed tame and commonplace. These two, living the actual scene, with all the deep, strong, real emotions of them surging to the surface, the vitality of them, all aroused and vibrating, suddenly confronting actuality itself, were not even natural; were not even " true to life." It was as though they had parted but a fortnight ago.

Bennett caught his cap from his head and came toward her, exclaiming:

"Miss Searight, I believe."

And she, reaching her right hand over the left, that still held the reins, leaned from her high seat, shaking hands with him and replying:

"Well—Mr. Bennett, I'm so very glad to see you again. Where did you come from?"

"From the City—and from seventy-six degrees north latitude."

"I congratulate you. We had almost given up hope of you."

"Thank you," he answered. "We were not so roseate with hope ourselves—all the time. But I have not felt as though I had really come back until this—well, until I had reached—the road between Bannister and Fourth Lake, for instance," and his face relaxed to its characteristic grim smile.

"You reached it too late, then," she responded. "Your dog has killed our Dan, and, what is much worse, started to eat him. He's a perfect savage."

"Kamiska? Well," he added, reflectively, "it's my fault for setting her a bad example. I ate her trace-mate, and was rather close to eating Kamiska herself at one time. But I didn't come down here to talk about that."

"You are looking rather worn, Mr. Bennett."

"I suppose. The doctor sent me into the country to call back the roses to my pallid cheek. So I came down here—to geologise. I presume that excuse will do as well as another." Then suddenly he cried: "Hello, steady there; *quick*, Miss Searight!"

It all came so abruptly that neither of them could afterward reconstruct the scene with any degree of accuracy. Probably in scrambling down the steep slope of the bank Bennett had loosened the earth or smaller stones that hitherto had been barely sufficient support to the mass of earth, gravel, rocks, and bushes that all at once, and with a sharp, crackling noise, slid downward toward the road from the overhanging bank. The slip was small, hardly more than three square yards of earth moving from its place, but it came with a smart, quick rush, throwing up a cloud of dust and scattering pebbles and hard clods of dirt far before its advance.

As Rox leaped Lloyd threw her weight too suddenly on the reins, the horse arched his neck, and the overhead check snapped like a harp-string. Again he reared from the object of his terror, shaking his head from side to side, trying to get a purchase on the bit. Then his lower jaw settled against his chest, and all at once he realised that no pair of human hands could hold him now. He did not rear again; his haunches suddenly lowered, and with the hoofs of his hind feet he began feeling the ground for his spring. But now Bennett was at his head, gripping at the bit, striving to thrust him back. Lloyd, half risen from her seat, each rein wrapped twice around her hands, her long, strong arms at their fullest reach, held back against the horse with all her might, her body swaying and jerking with his plunges. But the overhead check once broken Lloyd might as well have pulled against a locomotive. Bennett was a powerful man by nature, but his great strength had been not a little sapped by his recent experiences. Between the instant his hand caught at the bit and that

in which Rox had made his first ineffectual attempt
to spring forward he recognised the inequality of
the contest. He could hold Rox back for a second
or two, perhaps three, then the horse would get
away from him. He shot a glance about him. Not
twenty yards away was the canal and the perilously
narrow bridge—the bridge without the guard-rail.

"Quick, Miss Searight!" he shouted. "Jump!
We can't hold him. Quick, do as I tell you, jump!"

But even as he spoke Rox dragged him from his
feet, his hoofs trampling the hollow road till it
reverberated like the roll of drums. Bracing himself against every unevenness of the ground, his
teeth set, his face scarlet, the veins in his neck swelling, suddenly blue-black, Bennett wrenched at the
bit till the horse's mouth went bloody. But all to
no purpose; faster and faster Rox was escaping
from his control.

"Jump, I tell you!" he shouted again, looking
over his shoulder; "another second and he's away."

Lloyd dropped the reins and turned to jump. But
the lap-robe had slipped down to the bottom of the
cart when she had risen, and was in a tangle about
her feet. The cart was rocking like a ship in a
storm. Twice she tried to free herself, holding to
the dashboard with one hand. Then the cart suddenly lurched forward and she fell to her knees.
Rox was off; it was all over.

Not quite. In one brief second of time—a hideous vision come and gone between two breaths—
Lloyd saw the fearful thing done there in the road,
almost within reach of her hand. She saw the man
and horse at grapples, the yellow reach of road that

lay between her and the canal, the canal itself, and the narrow bridge. Then she saw the short-handled geologist's hammer gripped in Bennett's fist heave high in the air. Down it came, swift, resistless, terrible—one blow. The cart tipped forward as Rox, his knees bowing from under him, slowly collapsed. Then he rolled upon the shaft that snapped under him, and the cart vibrated from end to end as a long, shuddering tremble ran through him with his last deep breath.

V.

When Lloyd at length managed to free herself and jump to the ground Bennett came quickly toward her and drew her away to the side of the road.

"Are you hurt?" he demanded. "Tell me, are you hurt?"

"No, no; not in the least."

"Why in the world did you want to drive such a horse? Don't ever take such chances again. I won't have it."

For a few moments Lloyd was too excited to trust herself to talk, and could only stand helplessly to one side, watching Bennett as he stripped off the harness from the dead horse, stowed it away under the seat of the cart, and rolled the cart itself to the edge of the road. Then at length she said, trying to smile and to steady her voice:

"It—it seems to me, Mr. Bennett, you do about —about as you like with my sta-bub-ble."

"Sit down!" he commanded, "you are trembling all over. Sit down on that rock there."

"—— and with me," she added, sinking down upon the boulder he had indicated with a movement of his head, his hands busy with the harness.

"I'm sorry I had to do that," he explained; "but there was no help for it—nothing else to do. He

104

would have had you in the canal in another second, if he did not kill you on the way there."

" Poor old Rox," murmured Lloyd; " I was very fond of Rox."

Bennett put himself in her way as she stepped forward. He had the lap-robe over his arm and the whip in his hand.

" No, don't look at him. He's not a pretty sight. Come, shall I take you home? Don't worry about the cart; I will see that it is sent back."

" And that Rox is buried—somewhere? I don't want him left out there for the crows." In spite of Bennett's injunction she looked over her shoulder for a moment as they started off down the road. " I only hope you were sure there was nothing else to do, Mr. Bennett," she said.

" There was no time to think," he answered, " and I wasn't taking any chances."

But the savagery of the whole affair stuck in Lloyd's imagination. There was a primitiveness, a certain hideous simplicity in the way Bennett had met the situation that filled her with wonder and with even a little terror and mistrust of him. The vast, brutal directness of the deed was out of place and incongruous at this end-of-the-century time. It ignored two thousand years of civilisation. It was a harsh, clanging, brazen note, powerful, un-complicated, which came jangling in, discordant and inharmonious with the tune of the age. It savoured of the days when men fought the brutes with their hands or with their clubs. But also it was an indication of a force and a power of mind that stopped at nothing to attain its ends, that chose the

shortest cut, the most direct means, disdainful of
hesitation, holding delicacy and finessing in meas-
ureless contempt, rushing straight to its object,
driving in, breaking down resistance, smashing
through obstacles with a boundless, crude, blind
Brobdignag power, to oppose which was to be
trampled under foot upon the instant.

It was long before their talk turned from the incident of the morning, but when it did its subject
was Richard Ferriss. Bennett was sounding his
praises and commending upon his pluck and endurance during the retreat from the ship, when Lloyd,
after hesitating once or twice, asked:

" How is Mr. Ferriss? In your note you said he
was ill."

" So he is," he told her, " and I could not have
left him if I was not sure I was doing him harm by
staying. But the doctor is to wire me if he gets any
worse, and only if he does. I am to believe that
no news is good news."

But this meeting with Lloyd and the intense excitement of those few moments by the canal had
quite driven from Bennett's mind the fact that he
had *not* forwarded his present address either to
Ferriss or to his doctor. He had so intended that
morning, but all the faculties of his mind were suddenly concentrated upon another issue. For the
moment he believed that he had actually written to
Dr. Pitts, as he had planned, and when he thought
of his intended message at all, thought of it as an
accomplished fact. The matter did not occur to him
again.

As he walked by Lloyd's side, listening to her and

talking to her, snapping the whip the while, or flicking the heads from the mullein stalks by the roadside with its lash, he was thinking how best he might say to her what he had come from the City to say. To lead up to his subject, to guide the conversation, to prepare the right psychological moment skilfully and without apparent effort, were manœuvres in the game that Bennett ignored and despised. He knew only that he loved her, that she was there at his side, that the object of all his desires and hopes was within his reach. Straight as a homing pigeon he went to his goal.

"Miss Searight," he began, his harsh, bass voice pitched even lower than usual, "what do you think I am down here for? This is not the only part of the world where I could recuperate, I suppose, and as for spending God's day in chipping at stones, like a professor of a young ladies' seminary"—he hurled the hammer from him into the bushes—"that for geology! Now we can talk. You know very well that I love you, and I believe that you love me. I have come down here to ask you to marry me."

Lloyd might have done any one of a dozen things —might have answered in any one of a dozen ways. But what she did do, what she did say, took Bennett completely by surprise. A little coldly and very calmly she answered:

"You believe—you say you believe that I——" she broke off, then began again: "It is not right for you to say that to me. I have never led you to believe that I cared for you. Whatever our relations are to be, let us have that understood at once."

Bennett uttered an impatient exclamation. " I am not good at fencing and quibbling," he declared. " I tell you that I love you with all my heart. I tell you that I want you to be my wife, and I tell you that I know you do love me. You are not like other women; why should you coquette with me? Good God! are you not big enough to be above such things? I know you are. Of all the people in the world we two ought to be above pretence, ought to understand each other. If I did not know you cared for me I would not have spoken."

" I don't understand you," she answered. " I think we had better talk of other things this morning."

" I came down here to talk of just this and nothing else," he declared.

" Very well, then," she said, squaring her shoulders with a quick, brisk movement, " we *will* talk of it. You say we two should understand each other. Let us come to the bottom of things at once. I despise quibbling and fencing as much, perhaps, as you. Tell me how have I ever led you to believe that I cared for you? "

" At a time when our last hope was gone," answered Bennett, meeting her eyes, " when I was very near to death and thought that I should go to my God within the day, I was made happier than I think I ever was in my life before by finding out that I was dear to you—that you loved me."

Lloyd searched his face with a look of surprise and bewilderment.

" I do not understand you," she repeated.

A Man's Woman

" Oh ! " exclaimed Bennett with sudden vehemence, " you could say it to Ferriss; why can't you say it to me? "

" To Mr. Ferriss ? "

" You could tell *him* that you cared."

" I—tell Mr. Ferriss—that I cared for you? " She began to smile. " You are a little absurd, Mr. Bennett."

" And I cannot see why you should deny it now. Or if anything has caused you to change your mind —to be sorry for what you said, why should I not know it? Even a petty thief may be heard in his own defence. I loved you because I believed you to be a woman, a great, strong, noble, man's woman, above little things, above the little, niggling, contemptible devices of the drawing-room. I loved you because the great things of the world interested you, because you had no place in your life for petty graces, petty affectations, petty deceits and shams and insincerities. If you did not love me, why did you say so? If you do love me now, why should you not admit it? Do you think you can play with me? Do you think you can coquette with me? If you were small enough to stoop to such means, do you think I am small enough to submit to them? I have known Ferriss too well. I know him to be incapable of such falsity as you would charge him with. To have told such a lie, such an uncalled-for, useless, gratuitous lie, is a thing he could not have done. You must have told him that you cared. Why aren't you—you of all women—brave enough, strong enough, big enough to stand by your words? "

"Because I never said them. What do you think of me? Even if I did care, do you suppose I would say as much—and to another man? Oh!" she exclaimed with sudden indignation, "let's talk of something else. This is too—preposterous."

"You never told Ferriss that you cared for me?"

"No."

Bennett took off his cap. "Very well, then. That is enough. Good-bye, Miss Searight."

"Do you believe I told Mr. Ferriss I loved you?"

"I do not believe that the man who has been more to me than a brother is a liar and a rascal."

"Good-morning, Mr. Bennett."

They had come rather near to the farmhouse by this time. Without another word Bennett gave the whip and the lap-robe into her hands, and, turning upon his heel, walked away down the road.

Lloyd told Lewis as much of the morning's accident by the canal as was necessary, and gave orders about the dog-cart and the burying of Rox. Then slowly, her eyes fixed and wide, she went up to her own room and, without removing either her hat or her gloves, sat down upon the edge of the bed, letting her hands fall limply into her lap, gazing abstractedly at the white curtain just stirring at the open window.

She could not say which hurt her most—that Ferriss had told the lie or that Bennett believed it. But why, in heaven's name why, had Ferriss so spoken to Bennett; what object had he in view; what had he to gain by it? Why had Ferriss, the man who loved her, chosen so to humiliate her, to put her in a position so galling to her pride, her dignity? Bennett, too, loved her. How could he believe that she had so demeaned herself?

She had been hurt and to the heart, at a point where she believed herself most unassailable, and he who held the weapon was the man that with all the heart of her and soul of her she loved.

Much of the situation was all beyond her. Try as she would she could not understand. One thing, however, she saw clearly, unmistakably: Bennett believed that she loved him, believed that she had told as much to Ferriss, and that when she had denied all knowledge of Ferriss's lie she was only coquetting with him. She knew Bennett and his character well enough to realise that an idea once rooted in his mind was all but ineradicable. Bennett was not a man of easy changes; nothing mobile about him.

The thought of this belief of Bennett's was intolerable. As she sat there alone in her white room the dull crimson of her cheeks flamed suddenly scarlet, and with a quick, involuntary gesture she threw her hand, palm outward, across her face to hide it from the sunlight. She went quickly from one mood to another. Now her anger grew suddenly hot against Ferriss. How had he dared? How had he dared to put this indignity, this outrageous insult, upon her? Now her wrath turned upon Bennett. What audacity had been his to believe that she would so forget herself? She set her teeth in her impotent anger, rising to her feet, her hands clenching, tears of sheer passion starting to her eyes.

For the greater part of the afternoon she kept to

her room, pacing the floor from wall to wall, trying
to think clearly, to resolve upon something that
would readjust the situation, that would give her
back her peace of mind, her dignity, and her happiness of the early morning. For now the great joy
that had come to her in his safe return was all but
gone. For one moment she even told herself she
could not love him, but the next was willing to
admit that it was only because of her love of him,
as strong and deep as ever, that the humiliation cut
so deeply and cruelly now. Ferriss had lied about
her, and Bennett had believed the lie. To meet
Bennett again under such circumstances was not to
be thought of for one moment. Her vacation was
spoiled; the charm of the country had vanished.
Lloyd returned to the City the next day.

She found that she was glad to get back to her
work. The subdued murmur of the City that hourly
assaulted her windows was a relief to her ears after
the profound and numbing silence of the country.
The square was never so beautiful as at this time of
summer, and even the restless shadow pictures, that
after dark were thrown upon the ceiling of her room
by the electrics shining through the great elms in
the square below, were a pleasure.

On the morning after her arrival and as she was
unpacking her trunk Miss Douglass came into her
room and seated herself, according to her custom,
on the couch. After some half-hour's give-and-
take talk, the fever nurse said:

" Do you remember, Lloyd, what I told you about
typhoid in the spring—that it was almost epidemic? "

Lloyd nodded, turning about from her trunk, her arms full of dresses.

"It's worse than ever now," continued Miss Douglass; "three of our people have been on cases only in the short time you have been away. And there's a case out in Medford that has killed one nurse."

"Well!" exclaimed Lloyd in some astonishment, "it seems to me that one should confine typhoid easily enough."

"Not always, not always," answered the other; "a virulent case would be quite as bad as yellow fever or smallpox. You remember when we were at the hospital Miss Helmuth, that little Polish nurse, contracted it from her case and died even before her patient did. Then there was Eva Blayne. She very nearly died. I did like the way Miss Wakeley took this case out at Medford even when the other nurse had died. She never hesitated for——"

"Has one of our people got this case?" inquired Lloyd.

"Of course. Didn't I tell you?"

"I hope we cure it," said Lloyd, her trunk-tray in her hands. "I don't think we have ever lost a case yet when good nursing could pull it through, and in typhoid the whole treatment really is the nursing."

"Lloyd," said Miss Douglass decisively, "I would give anything I can think of now to have been on that hip disease case of yours and have brought my patient through as you did. You should hear what Dr. Street says of you—and the little girl's father. By the way, I had nearly forgotten. Hattie Campbell—that's her name, isn't it?—telephoned to know if you had come back from the country yet. That was yesterday. I said we expected you to-day, and she told me to say she was coming to see you."

The next afternoon toward three o'clock Hattie and her father drove to the square in an open carriage, Hattie carrying a great bunch of violets for Lloyd. The little invalid was well on the way to complete recovery by now. Sometimes she was allowed to walk a little, but as often as not her maid wheeled her about in an invalid's chair. She drove out in the carriage frequently by way of exercise. She would, no doubt, always limp a little, but in the end it was certain she would be sound and strong. For Hattie and her father Lloyd had become a sort of tutelary semi-deity. In what was left of the family she had her place, hardly less revered than even the dead wife. Campbell himself, who had made a fortune in Bessemer steel, a well-looking, well-groomed gentleman, smooth-shaven and with hair that was none too gray, more than once caught himself standing before Lloyd's picture that stood on the mantelpiece in Hattie's room, looking at it vaguely as he clipped the nib from his cigar.

But on this occasion as the carriage stopped in front of the ample pile of the house Hattie called out, "Oh, there she is now," and Lloyd came down the steps, carrying her nurse's bag in her hand.

"Are we too late?" began Hattie; "are you going out; are you on a case? Is that why you've got your bag? We thought you were on a vacation."

Campbell, yielding to a certain feeling of uneasiness that Lloyd should stand on the curb while he remained seated, got out of the carriage and stood at her side, gravely listening to the talk between the nurse and her one-time patient. Lloyd was obliged to explain, turning now to Hattie, now to her father. She told them that she was in something of a hurry. She had just been specially called to take a very bad case of typhoid fever in a little suburb of the City, called Medford. It was not her turn to go, but the physicians in charge of the case, as sometimes happened, had asked especially for her.

"One of our people, a young woman named Miss Wakeley, has been on this case," she continued, "but it seems she has allowed herself to contract the disease herself. She went to the hospital this noon."

Campbell, his gravity suddenly broken up, exclaimed:

"Surely, Miss Searight, this is not the same case I read of in yesterday's paper—it must be, too—Medford was the name of the place. That case has killed one nurse already, and now the second one is down. Don't tell me you are going to take the same case."

"It is the same case," answered Lloyd, "and, of course, I am going to take it. Did you ever hear of a nurse doing otherwise? Why, it would seem—seem so—funny——"

There was no dissuading her, and Campbell and Hattie soon ceased even to try. She was impatient to be gone. The station was close at hand, and she would not hear of taking the carriage thither. However, before she left them she recurred again to the subject of her letter to Mr. Campbell, and then and there it was decided that Hattie and her maid should spend the following ten days at Lloyd's place in Bannister. The still country air, now that Hattie was able to take the short journey, would be more to her than many medicines, and the ponies and Lloyd's phaëton would be left there with Lewis for her use.

"And write often, won't you, Miss Searight?" exclaimed Hattie as Lloyd was saying good-bye. Lloyd shook her head.

"Not that of all things," she answered. "If I did that we might have you, too, down with typhoid. But *you* may write to *me*, and I hope you will," and she gave Hattie her new address.

"Harriet," said Campbell as the carriage drove back across the square, the father and daughter waving their hands to Lloyd, briskly on her way to the railroad station, "Harriet."

"Yes, papa."

"There goes a noble woman. Pluck, intelligence, strong will—she has them all—and a great big heart that—heart that——" He clipped the end of a cigar thoughtfully and fell silent.

A day or two later, as Hattie was sitting in her little wheel-chair on the veranda of Mrs. Applegate's house watching Charley-Joe hunting grasshoppers underneath the currant bushes, she was surprised by the sharp closing of the front gate. A huge man with one squint eye and a heavy, square-cut jaw was coming up the walk, followed by a strange-looking dog. Charley-Joe withdrew swiftly to his particular hole under the veranda, moving rapidly, his body low to the ground, and taking an unnecessary number of very short steps.

The little city-bred girl distinguished the visitor from a country man at once. Hattie had ideas of her own as to propriety, and so rose to her feet as Bennett came up, and after a moment's hesitation made him a little bow. Bennett at once gravely took off his cap.

"Excuse me," he said as though Hattie were twenty-five instead of twelve. "Is Miss Searight at home?"

"Oh," exclaimed Hattie, delighted, "do you know Miss Searight? She was my nurse when I was so sick—because you know I had hip disease and there was an operation. No, she's not here any more. She's gone away, gone back to the City."

"Gone back to the City?"

"Yes, three or four days ago. But I'm going to write to her this afternoon. Shall I say who called?" Then, without waiting for a reply, she added, "I guess I had better introduce myself. My name is Harriet Campbell, and my papa is Craig V. Campbell, of the Hercules Wrought Steel Company in the City. Won't you have a chair?"

The little convalescent and the arctic explorer shook hands with great solemnity.

"I'm so pleased to meet you," said Bennett. "I haven't a card, but my name is Ward Bennett—of the Freja expedition," he added. But, to his relief, the little girl had not heard of him.

"Very well," she said, "I'll tell Miss Searight Mr. Bennett called."

"No," he replied, hesitatingly, "no, you needn't do that."

"Why, she won't answer my letter, you know," explained Hattie, "because she is afraid her letters would give me typhoid fever, that they might"—she continued carefully, hazarding a remembered phrase—"carry the con-ta-gion. You see she has gone to nurse a dreadful case of typhoid fever out at Medford, near the City, and we're so worried and anxious about her—papa and I. One nurse that had this case has died already and another one has caught the disease and is very sick, and Miss Searight, though she knew just how dangerous it was, *would* go, just like—like——" Hattie hesitated, then confused memories of her school reader coming to her, finished with "like Casabianca."

"Oh," said Bennett, turning his head so as to fix her with his own good eye. "She has gone to nurse a typhoid fever patient, has she?"

"Yes, and papa told me—" and Hattie became suddenly very grave, "that we might—might—oh, dear—never see her again."

"Hum! Whereabouts is this place in Medford? She gave you her address; what is it?" Hattie told him, and he took himself abruptly away.

Bennett had gone some little distance down the road before the real shock came upon him. Lloyd was in a position of imminent peril; her life was in the issue. With blind, unreasoned directness he leaped at once to this conclusion, and as he strode along with teeth and fists tight shut he kept muttering to himself: "She may die, she may die—we

—we may never see her again." Then suddenly came the fear, the sickening sink of heart, the choke at the throat, first the tightening and then the sudden relaxing of all the nerves. Lashed and harried by the sense of a fearful calamity, an unspeakable grief that was pursuing after him, Bennett did not stop to think, to reflect. He chose instantly to believe that Lloyd was near her death, and once the idea was fixed in his brain it was not thereafter to be reasoned away. Suddenly, at a turn in the road, he stopped, his hands deep in his pockets, his boot-heel digging into the ground. "Now, then," he exclaimed, "what's to be done?"

Just one thing: Lloyd must leave the case at once, that very day if it were possible. He must save her; must turn her back from this destruction toward which she was rushing, impelled by such a foolish, mistaken notion of duty.

"Yes," he said, "there's just that to be done, and, by God! it shall be done."

But would Lloyd be turned back from a course she had chosen for herself? Could he persuade her? Then with this thought of possible opposition Bennett's resolve all at once tightened to the sticking point. Never in the darkest hours of his struggle with the arctic ice had his determination grown so fierce; never had his resolution so girded itself, so nerved itself to crush down resistance. The force of his will seemed brusquely to be quadrupled and decupled. He would do as he desired; come what might he would gain his end. He would stop at nothing, hesitate at nothing. It would probably be difficult to get her from her post, but with all

his giant's strength Bennett set himself to gain her
safety.

A great point that he believed was in his favour,
a consideration that influenced him to adopt so irrevocable a resolution, was his belief that Lloyd
loved him. Bennett was not a woman's man. Men
he could understand and handle like so many mani-
kins, but the nature of his life and work did not con-
duce to a knowledge of women. Bennett did not
understand them. In his interview with Lloyd
when she had so strenuously denied Ferriss's story
Bennett could not catch the ring of truth. It had
gotten into his mind that Lloyd loved him. He
believed easily what he wanted to believe, and his
faith in Lloyd's love for him had become a part and
parcel of his fundamental idea of things, not readily
to be driven out even by Lloyd herself.

Bennett's resolution was taken. Never had he
failed in accomplishing that upon which he set his
mind. He would not fail now. Beyond a certain
limit—a limit which now he swiftly reached and
passed—Bennett's determination to carry his point
became, as it were, a sort of obsession; the sweep of
the tremendous power he unchained carried his own
self along with it in its resistless onrush. At such
times there was no light of reason in his actions.
He saw only his point, beheld only his goal; deaf to
all voices that would call him back, blind to all consideration that would lead him to swerve, reckless
of everything that he trampled under foot, he stuck
to his aim until that aim was an accomplished fact.
When the grip of the Ice had threatened to close
upon him and crush him, he had hurled himself

against its barriers with an energy and resolve to conquer that was little short of directed frenzy. So it was with him now.

.   .   .   .

When Lloyd had parted from the Campbells in the square before the house, she had gone directly to the railway station of a suburban line, and, within the hour, was on her way to Medford. As always happened when an interesting case was to be treated, her mind became gradually filled with it to the exclusion of everything else. The Campbells, and Bennett's ready acceptance of a story that put her in so humiliating a light, were forgotten as the train swept her from the heat and dust of the City out into the green reaches of country to the south-ward. What had been done upon the case she had no means of telling. She only knew that the case was of unusual virulence and well advanced. It had killed one nurse already and seriously endangered the life of another, but so far from reflecting on the danger to herself, Lloyd felt a certain exhilaration in the thought that she was expected to succeed where others had succumbed. Another battle with the Enemy was at hand, the Enemy who, though conquered on a hundred fields, must inevitably triumph in the end. Once again this Enemy had stooped and caught a human being in his cold grip. Once again Life and Death were at grapples, and Death was strong, and from out the struggle a cry had come—had come to her—a cry for help.

All the exuberance of battle grew big within her breast. She was impatient to be there—there at hand—to face the Enemy again across the sick-bed, where she had so often faced and outfought him before; and, matching her force against his force, her obstinacy against his strength—the strength that would pull the life from her grasp—her sleepless vigilance against his stealth, her intelligence against his cunning, her courage against his terrors, her resistance against his attack, her skill against his strategy, her science against his world-old, world-wide experience, win the fight, save the life, hold firm against his slow, resistless pull and triumph again, if it was only for the day.

Succeed she would and must. Her inborn obstinacy, her sturdy refusal to yield her ground, whatever it should be, her stubborn power of resistance, her tenacity of her chosen course, came to her aid as she drew swiftly near to the spot whereon the battle would be fought. Mentally she braced herself, holding back with all her fine, hard-tempered, native strength. No, she would not yield the life to the Enemy; no, she would not give up; no, she would not recede. Let the Enemy do his worst— she was strong against his efforts.

At Medford, which she reached toward four in the afternoon, after an hour's ride from the City, she found a conveyance waiting for her, and was driven rapidly through streets bordered with villas and closely shaven lawns to a fair-sized country seat on the outskirts of the town. The housekeeper met her at the door with the information that the doctor was, at the moment, in the sick-room, and had left orders that the nurse should be brought to him the moment she arrived. The housekeeper showed Lloyd the way to the second landing, knocking upon the half-open door at the end of the hall, and ushering her in without waiting for an answer.

Lloyd took in the room at a glance—the closely drawn curtains, the screen between the bed and the windows, the doctor standing on the hearth-rug, and the fever-inflamed face of the patient on the pillow. Then all her power of self-repression could not keep her from uttering a smothered exclamation.

For she, the woman who, with all the savage energy of him, Bennett loved, had, at peril of her life, come to nurse Bennett's nearest friend, the man of all others dear to him—Richard Ferriss.

VI.

Two days after Dr. Pitts had brought Ferriss to his country house in the outskirts of Medford he had been able to diagnose his sickness as typhoid fever, and at once had set about telegraphing the fact to Bennett. Then it had occurred to him that he did not know where Bennett had gone. Bennett had omitted notifying him of his present whereabouts, and, acting upon Dr. Pitts's advice, had hidden himself away from everybody. Neither at his club nor at his hotel, where his mail accumulated in extraordinary quantities, had any forwarding address been left. Bennett would not even know that Ferriss had been moved to Medford. So much the worse. It could not be helped. There was nothing for the doctor to do but to leave Bennett in ignorance and go ahead and fight for the life of Ferriss as best he could. Pitts arranged for a brother physician to take over his practice, and devoted himself entirely to Ferriss. And Ferriss sickened and sickened, and went steadily from bad to worse. The fever advanced regularly to a certain stage, a stage of imminent danger, and there paused. Rarely had Pitts been called upon to fight a more virulent form of the disease.

What made matters worse was that Ferriss hung on for so long a time without change one way or another. Pitts had long since been convinced of ulceration in the membrane of the intestines, but it astonished him that this symptom persisted so long without signs either of progressing or diminishing. The course of the disease was unusually slow. The first nurse had already had time to sicken and die; a second had been infected, and yet Ferriss " hung on," neither sinking nor improving, yet at every hour lying perilously near death. It was not often that death and life locked horns for so long, not often that the chance was so even. Many was the hour, many was the moment, when a hair would have turned the balance, and yet the balance was preserved.

At her abrupt recognition of Ferriss, in this patient whom she had been summoned to nurse, and whose hold upon life was so pitifully weak, Lloyd's heart gave a great leap and then sank ominously in her breast. Her first emotion was one of boundless self-reproach. Why had she not known of this? Why had she not questioned Bennett more closely as to his friend's sickness? Might she not have expected something like this? Was not typhoid the one evil to be feared and foreseen after experiences such as Ferriss had undergone—the fatigue and privations of the march over the ice, and the subsequent months aboard the steam whaler, with its bad food, its dirt, and its inevitable overcrowding?

And while she had been idling in the country, this man, whom she had known since her girlhood better and longer than any of her few acquaintances, had been struck down, and day by day had weakened and sickened and wasted, until now, at any hour, at any moment, the life might be snuffed out like the light of a spent candle. What a miserable incompetent had she been! That day in the park when she had come upon him, so weak and broken and far spent, why had she not, with all her training and experience, known that even then the flame was flickering down to the socket, that a link in the silver chain was weakening? Now, perhaps, it was too late. But quick her original obstinacy rose up in protest. No! she would not yield the life. No, no, no; again and a thousand times no! He belonged to her. Others she had saved, others far less dear to her than Ferriss. Her last patient—the little girl—she had caught back from death at the eleventh hour, and of all men would she not save Ferriss? In such sickness as this it was the nurse and not the doctor who must be depended upon. And, once again, never so strong, never so fine, never so glorious, her splendid independence, her pride in her own strength, her indomitable self-reliance leaped in her breast, leaped and stood firm, hard as tempered steel, head to the Enemy, daring the assault, defiant, immovable, unshaken in its resolve, unconquerable in the steadfast tenacity of its purpose.

The story that Ferriss had told to Bennett, that uncalled-for and inexplicable falsehood, was a thing forgotten. Death stood at the bedhead, and in that room the little things of life had no place. The king was holding court, and the swarm of small, every-day issues, like a crowd of petty courtiers, were not admitted to his presence. Ferriss's life was in danger. Lloyd saw no more than that. At once she set about the work.

In a few rapid sentences exchanged in low voices between her and the doctor Lloyd made herself acquainted with the case.

"We've been using the ice-pack and wet-pack to bring down the temperature in place of the cold bath," the doctor explained. "I'm afraid of pericarditis."

"Quinine?" inquired Lloyd.

"From twenty to forty grains in the morning and evening. Here's the temperature chart for the last week. If we reach this point in axilla again—" he indicated one hundred and two degrees with a thumb-nail—"we'll have to risk the cold bath, but only in that case."

"And the tympanites?"

Dr. Pitts put his chin in the air.

"Grave—there's an intestinal ulcer, no doubt of it, and if it perforates—well, we can send for the undertaker then."

"Has he had hæmorrhages?"

"Two in the first week, but not profuse—he seemed to rally fairly well afterward. We have been injecting ether in case of anæmia. Really, Miss Searight, the case is interesting, but wicked, wicked as original sin. Killed off my first nurse out of hand—good little boy, conscientious enough; took no care of himself; ate his meals in the sick-room against my wishes; off he went—dicrotic pulse, diarrhœa, vomiting, hospital, thrombosis of pulmonary artery, *pouf*, requiescat."

"And Miss Wakeley?"

"Knocked under yesterday, and she was fairly saturated with creolin night and morning. I don't know how it happened. . . . Well, God for us all. Here he is—that's the point for us." He glanced toward the bed, and for the third time Lloyd looked at the patient.

Ferriss was in a quiet delirium, and, at intervals, from behind his lips, dry and brown and fissured, there came the sounds of low and indistinct muttering. Barring a certain prominence of the cheekbones, his face was not very wasted, but its skin was a strange, dusky pallor. The cold pack was about his head like a sort of caricatured crown.

"Well," repeated Pitts in a moment, " I've been waiting for you to come to get a little rest. Was up all last night. Suppose you take over charge."

Lloyd nodded her head, removing her hat and gloves, making herself ready. Pitts gave her some final directions, and left her alone in the sick-room. For the moment there was nothing to do for the patient. Lloyd put on her hospital slippers and moved silently about the room, preparing for the night, and making some few changes in the matter of light and ventilation. Then for a while the medicine occupied her attention, and she was at some pains to carefully sort out the antiseptic and disinfectants from the drugs themselves. These latter she arranged on a table by themselves—studying the labels—assuring herself of their uses. Quinine for the regular morning and evening doses, sulphonal and trional for insomnia, ether for injections in case of anæmia after hæmorrhage, morphine for delirium, citrite of caffein for weakness of the heart, tincture of valerian for the tympanites, bismuth to relieve nausea and vomiting, and the crushed ice wrapped in flannel cloths for the cold pack in the event of hyperpyrexia.

Later in the evening she took the temperature in the armpit, noted the condition of the pulse, and managed to get Ferriss—still in his quiet, muttering delirium—to drink a glass of peptonised milk. She administered the quinine, reading the label, as was her custom, three times, once as she took it up, again as she measured the dose, and a last time as she returned the bottle to its place. Everything she did, every minute change in Ferriss's condition, she entered upon a chart, so that in the morning when Dr. Pitts should relieve her he could grasp the situation at a glance.

The night passed without any but the expected variations of the pulse and temperature, though toward daylight Lloyd could fancy that Ferriss, for a few moments, came out of his delirium and was conscious of his surroundings. For a few seconds his eyes seemed to regain something of their intelligence, and his glance moved curiously about the room. But Lloyd, sitting near the footboard of the bed, turned her head from him. It was not expedient that Ferris should recognise her now.

Lloyd could not but commend the wisdom of bringing Ferriss to Dr. Pitts's own house in so quiet a place as Medford. The doctor risked nothing. He was without a family, the only other occupants of the house being the housekeeper and cook. On more than one occasion, when an interesting case needed constant watching, Pitts had used his house as a sanatorium. Quiet as the little village itself was, the house was removed some little distance from its outskirts. The air was fine and pure. The stillness, the calm, the unbroken repose, was almost Sabbath-like. In the early watches of the night, just at the turn of the dawn, Lloyd heard the faint rumble of a passing train at the station nearly five miles away. For hours that and the prolonged stridulating of the crickets were the only sounds. Then at last, while it was yet dark, a faint chittering of waking birds began from under the eaves and from the apple-trees in the yard about the house. Lloyd went to the window, and, drawing aside the curtains, stood there for a moment looking out. She could see part of the road leading to the town, and, in the distance, the edge of the town itself, a few well-kept country residences of suburban dwellers of the City, and, farther on, a large, rectangular, brick building with cupola and flagstaff, perhaps the public school or the bank or the Odd Fellows' Hall. Nearer by were fields and corners of pasture land, with here and there the formless shapes of drowsing cows. One of these, as Lloyd watched, changed position, and she could almost hear the long, deep breath that accompanied the motion. Far off, miles upon miles, so it seemed, a rooster was crowing at exact intervals. All at once, and close at hand, another answered—a gay, brisk carillon that woke the echoes in an instant. For the first time Lloyd noticed a pale, dim belt of light low in the east.

Toward eight o'clock in the morning the doctor came to relieve her, and while he was examining the charts and she was making her report for the night the housekeeper announced breakfast.

" Go down to your breakfast, Miss Searight," said the doctor. " I'll stay here the while. The housekeeper will show you to your room."

But before breakfasting Lloyd went to the room the housekeeper had set apart for her—a different one than had been occupied by either of the previous nurses—changed her dress, and bathed her face and hands in a disinfecting solution. When she came out of her room the doctor met her in the hall; his hat and stick were in his hand. " He has gone to sleep," he informed her, " and is resting quietly. I am going to get a mouthful of fresh air along the road. The housekeeper is with him. If he wakes she'll call you. I will not be gone fifteen minutes. I've not been out of the house for five days, and there's no danger."

Breakfast had been laid in what the doctor spoke of as the glass-room. This was an enclosed veranda, one side being of glass and opening by French windows directly upon a little lawn that sloped away under the apple-trees to the road. It was a charming apartment, an idea of a sister of Dr. Pitts, who at one time had spent two years at Medford. Lloyd breakfasted here alone, and it was here that Bennett found her.

The one public carriage of Medford, a sort of four-seated carryall, that met all the trains at the depot, had driven to the gate at the foot of the yard, and had pulled up, the horses reeking and blowing. Even before it had stopped, a tall, square-shouldered man had alighted, but it was not until he was half-way up the gravel walk that Lloyd had recognised him. Bennett caught sight of her at the same

moment, and strode swiftly across the lawn and came
into the breakfast-room by one of the open French
windows. At once the room seemed to shrink in
size; his first step upon the floor—a step that was
almost a stamp, so eager it was, so masterful and
resolute—set the panes of glass jarring in their
frames. Never had Bennett seemed more out of
place than in this almost dainty breakfast-room,
with its small, feminine appurtenances, its fragile
glassware, its pots of flowers and growing plants.
The incongruous surroundings emphasized his
every roughness, his every angularity. Against its
background of delicate, mild tints his figure loomed
suddenly colossal; the great span of his chest and
shoulders seemed never so huge. His face; the
great, brutal jaw, with its aggressive, bullying, forward thrust; the close-gripped lips, the contracted
forehead, the small eyes, marred with the sharply
defined cast, appeared never so harsh, never so massive, never so significant of the resistless, crude force
of the man, his energy, his overpowering determination. As he towered there before her, one hand
gripped upon a chair-back, it seemed to her that
the hand had but to close to crush the little var-
nished woodwork to a splinter, and when he spoke
Lloyd could imagine that the fine, frail china of
the table vibrated to the deep-pitched bass of his
voice.

Lloyd had only to look at him once to know that
Bennett was at the moment aroused and agitated to
an extraordinary degree. His face was congested
and flaming. Under his frown his eyes seemed
flashing veritable sparks; his teeth were set; in his

temple a vein stood prominent and throbbing. But
Lloyd was not surprised. Bennett had, no doubt,
heard of Ferriss's desperate illness. Small wonder
he was excited when the life of his dearest friend
was threatened. Lloyd could ignore her own quarrel with Bennett at such a moment.

"I am so sorry," she began, "that you could not
have known sooner. But you remember you left
no address. There was——"

"What are you doing here?" he broke in
abruptly. "What is the use—why—" he paused
for a moment to steady his voice— "you can't stay
here," he went on. "Don't you know the risk you
are running? You can't stay here another moment."

"That," answered Lloyd, smiling, "is a matter
that is interesting chiefly to me. I suppose you
know that, Mr. Bennett."

"I know that you are risking your life and——"

"And that, too, is my affair."

"I have made it mine," he responded quickly.
"Oh," he exclaimed sharply, striking the back of
the chair with his open palm, "why must we always
be at cross-purposes with each other? I'm not
good at talking. What is the use of tangling ourselves with phrases? I love you, and I've come out
here to ask you, to beg you, you understand, to
leave this house, where you are foolishly risking
your life. You must do it," he went on rapidly. "I
love you too well. Your life is too much to me to
allow you to hazard it senselessly, foolishly. There
are other women, other nurses, who can take your
place. But you are not going to stay here."

Lloyd felt her indignation rising.

"This is my profession," she answered, trying to keep back her anger. "I am here because it is my duty to be here." Then suddenly, as his extraordinary effrontery dawned upon her, she exclaimed, rising to her feet: "Do I need to explain to you what I do? I am here because I choose to be here. That is enough. I don't care to go any further with such a discussion as this."

"You will not leave here, then?"

"No."

Bennett hesitated an instant, searching for his words, then:

"I do not know how to ask favours. I've had little experience in that sort of thing. You must know how hard it is for me, and you must understand to what lengths I am driven then, when I entreat you, when I beg of you, as humbly as it is possible for me to do so, to leave this house, now—at once. There is a train to the City within the hour; some one else can take your place before noon. We can telegraph; will you go?"

"You are absurd."

"Lloyd, can't you see; don't you understand? It's as though I saw you rushing toward a precipice with your eyes shut."

"My place is here. I shall not leave."

But Bennett's next move surprised her. His eagerness, his agitation left him upon the instant. He took out his watch.

"I was wrong," he said quietly. "The next train will not go for an hour and a quarter. There is more time than I supposed." Then, with as much

gentleness as he could command, he added:
" Lloyd, you are going to take that train ? "

" Now, you are becoming a little more than
absurd," she answered. " I don't know, Mr. Bennett, whether or not you intend to be offensive, but
I think you are succeeding rather well. You came
to this house uninvited; you invade a gentleman's
private residence, and you attempt to meddle and to
interfere with me in the practice of my profession.
If you think you can impress me with heroics and
declamation, please correct yourself at once. You
have only succeeded in making yourself a little
vulgar."

" That may be true or not," he answered with an
indifferent movement of his shoulders. " It is all
one to me. I have made up my mind that you shall
leave this house this morning, and believe me, Miss
Searight, I shall carry my point."

For the moment Lloyd caught her breath. For
the moment she saw clearly with just what sort of
man she had to deal. There was a conviction in
his manner—now that he had quieted himself—that
suddenly appeared unanswerable. It was like the
slow, still moving of a piston.

But the next moment her own character reas-
serted itself. She remembered what she was herself. If he was determined, she was obstinate; if
he was resolved, she was stubborn; if he was powerful, she was unyielding. Never had she conceded
her point before; never had she allowed herself to be
thwarted in the pursuance of a course she believed
to be right. Was she, of all women, to yield now?
The consciousness of her own power of resistance

came suddenly to her aid. Bennett was strong, but
was she not strong herself? Where under the blue
sky was the power that could break down her will?
When death itself could not prevail against her,
what in life could shake her resolution?

Suddenly the tremendous import of the moment,
the magnitude of the situation, flashed upon Lloyd.
Both of them had staked everything upon this issue.
Two characters of extraordinary power clashed
violently together. There was to be no compromise, no half-measures. Either she or Bennett
must in the end be beaten. One of them was to be
broken and humbled beyond all retrieving. There
in that commonplace little room, with its trivial
accessories, its inadequate background, a battle
royal swiftly prepared itself. With the abruptness
of an explosion the crisis developed.

"Do I need to tell you," remarked Bennett, "that
your life is rather more to me than any other consideration in the world? Do you suppose when the
lives of every member of my command depended
upon me I was any less resolved to succeed than I
am now? I succeeded then, and I shall succeed
now, now when there is much more at stake. I am
not accustomed to failure, and I shall not fail now.
I assure you that I shall stop at nothing."

It was beyond Lloyd to retain her calmness
under such aggression. It seemed as though
her self-respect demanded that she should lose her
temper.

"And you think you can drive me as you drove
your deck-hands?" she exclaimed. "What have
you to do with me? Am I your subordinate? Do

you think you can bully me? We are not in Kolyuchin Bay, Mr. Bennett."

"You're the woman I love," he answered with
an abrupt return of vehemence, "and, by God! I
shall stop at nothing to save your life."

"And my love for you, that you pretend is so
much to you, I suppose that this is the means you
take to awaken it. Admitting, for the moment,
that you could induce me to shirk my duty, how
should I love you for it? Ask yourself that."

But Bennett had but one answer to all her words.
He struck his fist into the palm of his hand as he
answered:

"Your life is more to me than any other consideration."

"But my life—how do you know it is a question
of my life? Come, if we are to quarrel, let us quarrel upon reasonable grounds. It does not follow
that I risk my life by staying——"

"Leave the house first; we can talk of that afterward."

"I have allowed you to talk too much already,"
she exclaimed angrily. "Let us come to the bottom of things at once. I will not be influenced nor
cajoled nor bullied into leaving my post. Now, *do*
you understand? That is my final answer. You
who were a commander, who were a leader of men,
what would you have done if one of your party had
left his post at a time of danger? I can tell you
what you would have done—you would have shot
him, after first disgracing him, and now you would
disgrace me. Is it reasonable? Is it consistent?"

Bennett snapped his fingers.

" That for consistency ! "

" And you would be willing to disgrace me—to
have me disgrace myself ? "

" Your life——" began Bennett again.

But suddenly Lloyd flashed out upon him with:
" My life! My life! Are there not some things
better than life? You, above all men, should understand that much. Oh, be yourself, be the man I
thought you were. You have your code; let me
have mine. You could not be what you are, you
could not have done what you did, if you had not
set so many things above merely your life. Admit
that you could not have loved me unless you believed that I could do the same. How could you
still love me if you knew I had failed in my duty?
How could you still love me if you knew that you
had broken down my will? I know you better than
you know yourself. You loved me because you
knew me to be strong and brave and to be above
petty deceptions and shams and subterfuges. And
now you ask me to fail, to give up, to shirk, and you
tell me you do so because you love me."

" That is all so many words to me. I cannot
argue with you, and there is no time for it. I did
not come here to—converse."

Never in her life before had Lloyd been so angry
as at that moment. The sombre crimson of her
cheeks had suddenly given place to an unwonted
paleness; even her dull-blue eyes, that so rarely
sparkled, were all alight. She straightened herself.

" Very well, then," she answered quietly, " our
conversation can stop where it is. You will excuse

me, Mr. Bennett, if I leave you. I have my work
to do."

Bennett was standing between her and the door.,
He did not move. Very gravely he said:

"Don't. Please don't bring it—to that."

Lloyd flashed a look at him, her eyes wide, exclaiming:

"You don't mean—you don't dare——"

"I tell you again that I mean to carry my point."

"And I tell you that I shall *not* leave my patient."

Bennett met her glance for an instant, and, holding her gaze with his, answered but two words.
Speaking in a low voice and with measured slow-
ness, he said:

"You—shall."

There was a silence. The two stood there, looking straight into one another's eyes, their mutual
opposition at its climax. The seconds began to
pass. The conflict between the man's aggression
and the woman's resistance reached its turning
point. Before another word should be spoken, before the minute should pass, one of the two must
give ground.

And then it was that Lloyd felt something break-
down within her, something to which she could
not put a name. A mysterious element of her character, hitherto rigid and intact, was beginning at
last to crumble. Somewhere a breach had been
opened; somewhere the barrier had been undermined. The fine steadfastness that was hers, and
that she had so dearly prized, her strength in which
she had gloried, her independence, her splendid

arrogant self-confidence and conscious power seemed all at once to weaken before this iron resolve that shut its ears and eyes, this colossal, untutored, savage intensity of purpose.

And abruptly her eyes were opened, and the inherent weakness of her sex became apparent to her. Was it a mistake, then? Could not a woman be strong? Was her strength grafted upon elemental weakness—not her individual weakness, but the weakness of her sex, the intended natural weakness of the woman? Had she built her fancied impregnable fortress upon sand?

But habit was too strong. For an instant, brief as the opening and shutting of an eye, a vision was vouchsafed to her, one of those swift glimpses into unplumbed depths that come sometimes to the human mind in the moments of its exaltation, but that are gone with such rapidity that they may not be trusted. For an instant Lloyd saw deep down into the black, mysterious gulf of sex—down, down, down where, immeasurably below the world of little things, the changeless, dreadful machinery of Life itself worked, clashing and resistless in its grooves. It was a glimpse fortunately brief, a vision that does not come too often, lest reason, brought to the edge of the abyss, grow giddy at the sight and, reeling, topple headlong. But quick the vision passed, the gulf closed, and she felt the firm ground again beneath her feet.

" I shall not," she cried.

Was it the same woman who had spoken but one moment before? Did her voice ring with the same undaunted defiance? Was there not a note of despair in her tones, a barely perceptible quaver, the symbol of her wavering resolve? Was not the very fact that she must question her strength proof positive that her strength was waning?

But her courage was unshaken, even if her strength was breaking. To the last she would strive, to the end she would hold her forehead high. Not till the last hope had been tried would she acknowledge her defeat.

"But in any case," she said, "risk is better than certainty. If I risk my life by staying, it is certain that he will die if I leave him at this critical moment."

"So much the worse, then—you cannot stay."

Lloyd stared at him in amazement.

"It isn't possible; I don't believe you can understand. Do you know how sick he is? Do you know that he is lying at the point of death at this very moment, and that the longer I stay away from him the more his life is in peril? Has he not rights as well as I; has he not a right to live? It is not only my own humiliation that is at stake, it is the life of your dearest friend, the man who stood by you, and helped you, and who suffered the same hardships and privations as yourself."

"What's that?" demanded Bennett with a sudden frown.

"If I leave Mr. Ferriss now, if he is left alone here for so much as half an hour, I will not answer——"

"Ferriss! What are you talking about? What is your patient's name?"

"Didn't you know?"

"Ferriss! Dick Ferriss! Don't tell me it's Dick Ferriss."

"I thought all the time you knew—that you had heard. Yes, it is Mr. Ferriss."

"Is he very sick? What is he doing out here? No, I had not heard; nobody told me. Pitts was to write—to—to wire. Will he pull through? What's the matter with him? Is it he who had typhoid?"

"He is very dangerously ill. Dr. Pitts brought him here. This is his house. We do not know if he will get well. It is only by watching him every instant that we can hope for anything. At this moment there is no one with him but a servant. *Now,* Mr. Bennett, am I to go to my patient?"

"But—but—we can get some one else."

"Not before three hours, and it's only the truth when I tell you he may die at any minute. Am I to go?"

In a second of time the hideous situation leaped up before Bennett's eyes. Right or wrong, the conviction that Lloyd was terribly imperilling her life by remaining at her patient's bedside had sunk into his mind and was not to be eradicated. It was a terror that had gripped him close and that could not be reasoned away. But Ferriss? What of him? Now it had brusquely transpired that his life, too, hung in the balance. How to decide? How to meet this abominable complication wherein he must sacrifice the woman he so dearly loved or the man who was the Damon to his Pythias, the Jonathan to his David?

"Am I to go?" repeated Lloyd for the third time.

Bennett closed his eyes, clasping his head with both hands.

" Great God, wait—wait—I can't think—I—I, oh, this is terrible ! "

Lloyd drove home her advantage mercilessly.

" Wait? I tell you we can't wait."

Then Bennett realised with a great spasm of horror that for him there was no going back. All his life, accustomed to quick decisions in moments of supreme peril, he took his decision now, facing, with such courage as he could muster, its unspeakable consequences, consequences that he knew must harry and hound him all the rest of his life. Whichever way he decided, he opened his heart to the beak and talons of a pitiless remorse. He could no longer see, in the dreadful confusion of his mind, the right of things or the wrong of things, could not accurately weigh chances or possibilities. For him only two alternatives presented themselves, the death of Ferriss or the death of Lloyd. He could see no compromise, could imagine no escape. It was as though a headsman with ready axe stood at his elbow, awaiting his commands. And, besides all this, he had long since passed the limit—though perhaps he did not know it himself—where he could see anything but the point he had determined to gain, the goal he had determined to reach. His mind was made up. His furious energy, his resolve to conquer at all costs, had become at last a sort of directed frenzy. The engine he had set in motion was now beyond his control. He could not now—whether he would or no—reverse its action, swerve it from its iron path, call it back from the monstrous catastrophe toward which it was speeding him.

" God help us all ! " he muttered.

" Well," said Lloyd expectantly.

Bennett drew a deep breath, his hands falling helplessly at his sides. In a way he appeared suddenly bowed; the great frame of bone and sinew seemed in some strange, indefinable manner to shrink, to stagger under the sudden assumption of an intolerable burden—a burden that was never to be lifted.

Even then, however, Bennett still believed in the wisdom of his course, still believed himself to be right. But, right or wrong, he now must go forward. Was it fate, was it doom, was it destiny?

Bennett's entire life had been spent in the working out of great ideas in the face of great obstacles; continually he had been called upon to overcome enormous difficulties with enormous strength. For long periods of time he had been isolated from civilisation, had been face to face with the simple, crude forces of an elemental world—forces that were to be combated and overthrown by means no less simple and crude than themselves. He had lost the faculty, possessed, no doubt, by smaller minds, of dealing with complicated situations. To resort to expedients, to make concessions, was all beyond him. For him a thing was absolutely right or absolutely wrong, and between the two there was no gradation. For so long a time had he looked at the larger, broader situations of life that his mental vision had become all deformed and confused. He saw things invariably magnified beyond all proportion, or else

dwarfed to a littleness that was beneath consideration. Normal vision was denied him. It was as
though he studied the world through one or the
other ends of a telescope, and when, as at present,
his emotions were aroused, matters were only made
the worse. The idea that Ferriss might recover,
though Lloyd should leave him at this moment,
hardly presented itself to his mind. He was convinced that if Lloyd went away Ferriss would die;
Lloyd had said as much herself. The hope that
Lloyd might, after all, nurse him through his sickness without danger to herself was so remote that
he did not consider it for one instant. If Lloyd
remained she, like the other nurse, would contract
the disease and die.

These were the half-way measures Bennett did
not understand, the expedients he could no longer
see. It was either Lloyd or Ferriss. He must
choose between them.

Bennett went to the door of the room, closed it
and leaned against it.

" No," he said.

Lloyd was stricken speechless. For the instant
she shrank before him as if from a murderer. Bennett now knew precisely the terrible danger in which
he left the man who was his dearest friend. Would
he actually consent to his death? It was almost beyond belief, and for the moment Lloyd herself
quailed before him. Her first thoughts were not of
herself, but of Ferriss. If he was Bennett's friend
he was her friend too. At that very moment he
might be dying for want of her care. She was fast
becoming desperate. For the moment she could

put all thought of herself and of her own dignity in the background.

"What is it you want?" she cried. "Is it my humiliation you ask? Well, then, you have it. It is as hard for me to ask favours as it is for you. I am as proud as you, but I entreat you, you hear me, as humbly as I can, to let me go. What do you want more than that? Oh, can't you understand? While we talk here, while you keep me here, he may be dying. Is it a time for arguments, is it a time for misunderstandings, is it a time to think of ourselves, of our own lives, our own little affairs?" She clasped her hands. "Will you please—can I, can I say more than that; will you please let me go?"

"No."

With a great effort Lloyd tried to regain her self-control. She paused a moment, then:

"Listen!" she said. "You say that you love me; that I am more to you than even Mr. Ferriss, your truest friend. I do not wish to think of myself at such a time as this, but supposing that you should make me—that I should consent to leave my patient. Think of me then, afterward. Can I go back there to the house, the house that I built? Can I face the women of my profession? What would they think of me? What would my friends think of me—I who have held my head so high? You will ruin my life. I should have to give up my profession. Oh, can't you see in what position you would place me?" Suddenly the tears sprang to her eyes. "No!" she cried vehemently. "No, no, no, I will not, I will not be disgraced!"

A Man's Woman

"I have no wish to disgrace you," answered Bennett. "It is strange for you to say that to me, if I love you so well that I can give up Ferriss for——"

"Then, if you love me so much as that, there must be one thing that you would set even above my life. Do you wish to make me hate you?"

"There is nothing in the world more to me than your life; you know that. How can you think it of me?"

"Because you don't understand—because you don't know that—oh, that I love you! I—no—I didn't mean—I didn't mean——"

What had she said? What had happened? How was it that the words that yesterday she would have been ashamed to so much as whisper to herself had now rushed to her lips almost of their own accord? After all those years of repression, suddenly the sweet, dim thought she had hidden in her secretest heart's heart had leaped to light and to articulate words. Unasked, unbidden, she had told him that she loved him. She, she had done this thing when, but a few moments before, her anger against him had shaken her to her very finger-tips. The hot, intolerable shame of it smote like fire into her face. Her world was cracking about her ears; everything she had prized the dearest was being torn from her, everything she had fancied the strongest was being overthrown. Had she, she who had held herself so proud and high, come at last to this?

Swiftly she turned from him and clasped her hands before her eyes and sank down into the chair she had quitted, bowing her head upon her arms, hiding her face, shutting herself from the light of

147

day, quivering and thrilling with an agony of shame
and with an utter, an abject self-contempt that was
beyond all power of expression. But the instant
she felt Bennett's touch upon her shoulder she
sprang up as if a knife had pierced her, and shrank
from him, turning her head away, her hand, palm
outward, before her eyes.

"Oh, please!" she begged piteously, almost in-
articulately in the stress of her emotion, "don't—
if you are a man—don't take advantage—please,
please don't touch me. Let me go away."

She was talking to deaf ears. In two steps Bennett had reached her side and had taken her in his
arms. Lloyd could not resist. Her vigour of body
as well as of mind was crushed and broken and
beaten down; and why was it that in spite of her
shame, that in spite of her unutterable self-reproach,
the very touch of her cheek upon his shoulder was a
comfort? Why was it that to feel herself carried
away in the rush of this harsh, impetuous, masculine
power was a happiness? Why was it that to know
that her prided fortitude and hitherto unshaken
power were being overwhelmed and broken with a
brutal, ruthless strength was an exultation and a
glory? Why was it that she who but a moment
before quailed from his lightest touch now put her
arms about his neck and clung to him with a sense
of protection and of refuge, the need of which she
had always and until that very moment disdained?

"Why should you be sorry because you spoke?"
said Bennett. "I knew that you loved me and you
knew that I loved you. What does it matter if you
said it or did not say it? We know each other, you

and I. We understand. You knew that I loved you. You think that I have been strong and determined, and have done the things I set out to do; what I am is what you made me. What I have done I have done because I thought you would approve. Do you think I would have come back if I had not known that I was coming back to you?" Suddenly an impatient exclamation escaped him, and his clasp about her tightened. "Oh! words— the mere things that one can *say*, seem so pitiful, so miserably inadequate. Don't you know, can't you feel what you are to me? Tell me, do you think I love you?"

But she could not bear to meet his glance just yet. Her eyes were closed, and she could only nod her head.

But Bennett took her head in both his hands and turned her face to his. Even yet she kept her eyes closed.

"Lloyd," he said, and his voice was almost a command; "Lloyd, look at me. Do you love me?"

She drew a deep breath. Then her sweet dull-blue eyes opened, and through the tears that brimmed them and wet her lashes she looked at him and met his glance fearlessly and almost proudly, and her voice trembled and vibrated with an infinite tenderness as she answered:

"I do love you, Ward; love you with all my heart."

Then, after a pause, she said, drawing a little from him and resting a hand upon either shoulder:

"But listen, dear; we must not think of ourselves now. We must think of him, so sick and weak and

helpless. This is a terrible moment in our lives.
I don't know why it has come to us. I don't know
why it should all have happened as it has this morning. Just a few moments ago I was angry as I
never was in my life before—and at you—and now
it seems to me that I never was so happy; I don't
know myself any more. Everything is confused;
all we can do is to hold to what we know is right
and trust that everything will be well in the end.
It is a crisis, isn't it? And all our lives and all our
happiness depend upon how we meet it. I am all
different now. I am not the woman I was a half-
hour ago. You must be brave for me now, and you
must be strong for me and help me to do my duty.
We must live up to the best that is in us and do
what we think is right, no matter what risks we run,
no matter what the consequences are. I would not
have asked you to help me before—before what has
happened—but now I need your help. You have
said I helped you to be brave; help me to be brave
now, and to do what I know is right."

But Bennett was still blind. If she had been dear
to him before, how doubly so had she become since
she had confessed her love for him! Ferriss was
forgotten, ignored. He could not let her go, he
could not let her run the slightest risk. Was he to
take any chance of losing her now? He shook his
head.

"Ward!" she exclaimed with deep and serious
earnestness. "If you do not wish me to risk my life
by going to my post, be careful, oh, be very careful,
that you do not risk something that is more to us
both than life itself, by keeping me from it. Do

you think I could love you so deeply and so truly as I do if I had not kept my standards high; if I had not believed in the things that were better than life, and stronger than death, and dearer to me than even love itself? There are some things I cannot do: I cannot be false, I cannot be cowardly, I cannot shirk my duty. Now I am helpless in your hands. You have conquered, and you can do with me as you choose. But if you make me do what is false, and what is cowardly, and what is dishonourable; if you stand between me and what I know is my duty, how can I love you, how can I love you?"

Persistently, perversely, Bennett stopped his ears to every consideration, to every argument. She wished to hazard her life. That was all he understood.

"No, Lloyd," he answered, "you must not do it."

"——and I want to love you," she went on, as though she had not heard. "I want you to be everything to me. I have trusted you so long—had faith in you so long, I don't want to think of you as the man who failed me when I most needed his help, who made me do the thing that was contemptible and unworthy. Believe me," she went on with sudden energy, "you will kill my love for you if you persist."

But before Bennett could answer there was a cry.

"It is the servant," exclaimed Lloyd quickly. "She has been watching—there in the room with him."

"Nurse—Miss Searight," came the cry, "quick—there is something wrong—I don't know—oh, hurry!"

"Do you hear?" cried Lloyd. "It is the crisis —he may be dying. Oh, Ward, it is the man you love! We can save him." She stamped her foot in the frenzy of her emotion, her hands twisting together. "I *will* go. I forbid you to keep—to hinder—to—to, oh, what is to become of us? If you love me, if you love him—*Ward, will you let me go?*"

Bennett put his hands over his ears, his eyes closed. In the horror of that moment, when he realised that no matter how he might desire it he could not waver in his resolution, it seemed to him that his reason must give way. But he set his back to the door, his hand gripped tight upon the knob, and through his set teeth his answer came as before:

"No."

"Nurse—Miss Searight, where are you? Hurry, oh, hurry!"

"Will you let me go?"

"No."

Lloyd caught at his hand, shut so desperately upon the knob, striving to loosen his clasp. She hardly knew what she was doing; she threw her arms about his neck, imploring, commanding, now submissive, now imperious, her voice now vibrating with anger, now trembling with passionate entreaty.

"You are not only killing him, you are killing my love for you; will you let me go—the love that is so dear to me? Let me love you, Ward; listen to me; don't make me hate you; let me love you, dear——"

"Hurry, oh, hurry!"

"Let me love you; let him live. I want to love

you. It's the best happiness in my life. Let me be happy. Can't you see what this moment is to mean for us? It is our happiness or wretchedness forever. Will you let me go?"

"No."

"For the last time, Ward, listen! It is my love for you and his life. Don't crush us both—yes, and yourself. You who can, who are so powerful, don't trample all our happiness under foot."

"Hurry, hurry; oh, will nobody come to help?"

"Will you let me go?"

"No."

Her strength seemed all at once to leave her. All the fabric of her character, so mercilessly assaulted, appeared in that moment to reel, topple, and go crashing to its wreck. She was shattered, broken, humbled, and beaten down to the dust. Her pride was gone, her faith in herself was gone, her fine, strong energy was gone. The pity of it, the grief of it; all that she held dearest; her fine and confident steadfastness; the great love that had brought such happiness into her life—that had been her inspiration, all torn from her and tossed aside like chaff. And her patient—Ferriss, the man who loved her, who had undergone such suffering, such hardship, who trusted her and whom it was her duty to nurse back to life and health—if he should perish for want of her care, then what infinite sorrow, then what endless remorse, then what long agony of unavailing regret! Her world, her universe grew dark to her; she was driven from her firm stand. She was lost, she was whirled away—away with the storm, landmarks obliterated, lights gone; away

with the storm; out into the darkness, out into the
void, out into the waste places and wilderness and
trackless desolation.

" Hurry, oh, hurry ! "

It was too late. She had failed; the mistake had
been made, the question had been decided. That
insensate, bestial determination, iron-hearted, iron-
strong, had beaten down opposition, had carried its
point. Life and love had been crushed beneath
its trampling without pity, without hesitation. The
tragedy of the hour was done; the tragedy of the
long years to come was just beginning.

Lloyd sank down in the chair before the table,
and the head that she had held so high bowed down
upon her folded arms. The violence of her grief
shook her from head to foot like a dry, light reed.
Her heart seemed literally to be breaking. She
must set her teeth with all her strength to keep from
groaning aloud, from crying out in her hopeless
sorrow her impotent shame and despair.

Once more came the cry for help. Then the
house fell silent. The minutes passed. But for
Lloyd's stifled grief there was no sound. Bennett—
leaning heavily against the door, his great shoulders
stooping and bent, his face ashen, his eyes fixed—
did not move. He did not speak to Lloyd. There
was no word of comfort he could address to her—
that would have seemed the last mockery. He had
prevailed, as he knew he should, as he knew he
must, when once his resolve was taken. The force
that, once it was unleashed, was beyond him to control, had accomplished its purpose. His will remained unbroken; but at what cost? However,

that was for future consideration. The costs? Had he not his whole life before him in which to count them? The present moment still called upon him to act. He looked at his watch.

The next quarter of an hour was all a confusion to him. Its incidents refused to define themselves upon his memory when afterward he tried to recall them. He could remember, however, that when he helped Lloyd into the carryall that was to take her to the depot in the village she had shrunk from his touch and had drawn away from him as if from a criminal—a murderer. He placed her satchel on the front seat with the driver, and got up beside the driver himself. She had drawn her veil over her face, and during the drive sat silent and motionless.

" Can you make it? " asked Bennett of the driver, watch in hand. The time was of the shortest, but the driver put the whip to his horses and, at a run, they reached the railway station a few moments ahead of time. Bennett told the driver to wait, and while Lloyd remained in her place he bought her ticket for the City. Then he went to the telegraph office and sent a peremptory despatch to the house on Calumet Square.

A few moments later the train had come and gone, an abrupt eruption of roaring iron and shrieking steam. Bennett was left on the platform alone, watching it lessen to a smoky blur where the rails converged toward the horizon. For an instant he stood watching, watching a resistless, iron-hearted force whirling her away, out of his reach, out of his life. Then he shook himself, turning sharply about.

"Back to the doctor's house, now," he commanded the driver; "on the run, you understand."

But the other protested. His horses were all but exhausted. Twice they had covered that distance at top speed and under the whip. He refused to return. Bennett took the young man by the arm and lifted him from his seat to the ground. Then he sprang to his place and lashed the horses to a gallop.

When he arrived at Dr. Pitts's house he did not stop to tie the horses, but threw the reins over their backs and entered the front hall, out of breath and panting. But the doctor, during Bennett's absence, had returned, and it was he who met him half-way up the stairs.

"How is he?" demanded Bennett. "I have sent for another nurse; she will be out here on the next train. I wired from the station."

"The only objection to that," answered the doctor, looking fixedly at him, "is that it is not necessary. Mr. Ferriss has just died."

VII.

Throughout her ride from Medford to the City it was impossible for Lloyd, so great was the confusion in her mind, to think connectedly. She had been so fiercely shocked, so violently shattered and weakened, that for a time she lacked the power and even the desire to collect and to concentrate her scattering thoughts. For the time being she felt, but only dimly, that a great blow had fallen, that a great calamity had overwhelmed her, but so extraordinary was the condition of her mind that more than once she found herself calmly awaiting the inevitable moment when the full extent of the catastrophe would burst upon her. For the moment she was merely tired. She was willing even to put off this reaction for a while, willing to remain passive and dizzied and stupefied, resigning herself helplessly and supinely to the swift current of events.

Yet while that part of her mind which registered the greater, deeper, and more lasting impressions remained inactive, the smaller faculty, that took cognisance of the little, minute-to-minute matters, was as busy and bright as ever. It appeared that the blow had been struck over this latter faculty, and not, as one so often supposes, through it. She seemed in that hour to understand the reasonableness of this phenomenon, that before had always appeared so inexplicable, and saw how great sorrow as well as great joy strikes only at the greater machinery of the brain, overpassing and ignoring the little wheels and cogs, that work on as briskly as ever in storm or calm, being moved only by temporary and trivial emotions and impressions.

So it was that for upward of an hour while the train carried her swiftly back to the City, Lloyd sat quietly in her place, watching the landscape rushing past her and cut into regular divisions by the telegraph poles like the whirling pictures of a kinetoscope. She noted, and even with some particularity, the other passengers—a young girl in a smart tailor-made gown reading a book, cutting the leaves raggedly with a hairpin; a well-groomed gentleman with a large stomach, who breathed loudly through his nose; the book agent with his oval boxes of dried figs and endless thread of talk; a woman with a little boy who wore spectacles and who was continually making unsteady raids upon the water-cooler, and the brakeman and train conductor laughing and chatting in the forward seat.

She took an interest in every unusual feature of the country through which the train was speeding, and noted each stop or increase of speed. She found a certain diversion, as she had often done before, in watching for the mile-posts and in keeping count of the miles. She even asked the conductor at what time the train would reach the City, and uttered a little murmur of vexation when she was told that it was a half-hour late. The next instant she was asking herself why this delay should seem annoying to her. Then, toward the close of the afternoon, came the City itself. First a dull-gray smudge on the horizon, then a world of grimy streets, rows of miserable tenements festooned with rags, then a tunnel or two, and at length the echoing glass-arched terminal of the station. Lloyd alighted, and, remembering that the distance was short, walked steadily toward her destination till the streets and neighbourhood became familiar. Suddenly she came into the square. Directly opposite was the massive granite front of the agency. She paused abruptly. She was returning to the house after abandoning her post. What was she to say to them, the other women of her profession?

Then all at once came the reaction. Instantly the larger machinery of the mind resumed its functions, the hurt of the blow came back. With a fierce wrench of pain, the wound reopened, full consciousness returned. Lloyd remembered then that she had proved false to her trust at a moment of danger, that Ferriss would probably die because of what she had done, that her strength of will and of mind wherein she had gloried was broken beyond redemption; that Bennett had failed her, that her love for him, the one great happiness of her life, was dead and cold and could never be revived, and that in the eyes of the world she stood dishonoured and disgraced.

Now she must enter that house, now she must face its inmates, her companions. What to say to them? How explain her defection? How tell them that she had not left her post of her own will? Lloyd fancied herself saying in substance that the man who loved her and whom she loved had made her abandon her patient. She set her teeth. No,

not that confession of miserable weakness; not that
of all things. And yet the other alternative, what
was that? It could be only that she had been
afraid—she, Lloyd Searight! Must she, who had
been the bravest of them all, stand before that little
band of devoted women in the light of a self-con-
fessed coward?

She remembered the case of the young English
woman, Harriet Freeze, who, when called upon to
nurse a smallpox patient, had been found wanting
in courage at the crucial moment, and had discovered an excuse for leaving her post. Miss Freeze
had been expelled dishonourably from the midst of
her companions. And now she, Lloyd, standing
apparently convicted of the same dishonour, must
face the same tribunal. There was no escape. She
must enter that house, she must endure that ordeal,
and this at precisely the time when her resolution
had been shattered, her will broken, her courage
daunted. For a moment the idea of flight suggested itself to her—she would avoid the issue. She
would hide from reproach and contumely, and without further explanation go back to her place in the
country at Bannister. But the little exigencies of
her position made this impossible. Besides her
nurse's bag, her satchel was the only baggage she
had at that moment, and she knew that there was
but little money in her purse.

All at once she realised that while debating the
question she had been sitting on one of the benches
under the trees in the square. The sun was setting;
evening was coming on. Maybe if she waited until
six o'clock she could enter the house while the other

nurses were at supper, gain her room unobserved, then lock herself in and deny herself to all callers. But Lloyd made a weary, resigned movement of her shoulders. Sooner or later she must meet them all eye to eye. It would be only putting off the humiliation.

She rose, and, turning to the house, began to walk slowly toward it. Why put it off? It would be as hard at one time as another. But so great was her sense of shame that even as she walked she fancied that the very passers-by, the loungers on the benches around the fountain, must know that here was a disgraced woman. Was it not apparent in her very face, in the very uncertainty of her gait? She told herself she had not done wisely to sit even for a moment upon the bench she had just quitted. She wondered if she had been observed, and furtively glanced about her. There! Was not that nursemaid studying her too narrowly? And the policeman close at hand, was he not watching her quizzically? She quickened her gait, moved with a sudden impulse to get out of sight, to hide within doors—where? In the house? There where, so soon as she set foot in it, her companions, the other nurses, must know her dishonour? Where was she to go? Where to turn? What was to become of her?

But she *must* go to the house. It was inevitable. She went forward, as it were, step by step. That little journey across the square under the elms and cottonwoods was for her a veritable *chemin de la croix*. Every step was an agony; every yard covered only brought her nearer the time and place of exposure. It was all the more humiliating because she knew that her impelling motive was not one of duty. There was nothing lofty in the matter— nothing self-sacrificing. She went back because she had to go back. Little material necessities, almost ludicrous in their pettiness, forced her on.

As she came nearer she looked cautiously at the windows of the agency. Who would be the first to note her home-coming? Would it be Miss Douglass, or Esther Thielman, or Miss Bergyn, the superintendent nurse? What would first be said to her? With what words would she respond? Then how the news of the betrayal of her trust would flash from room to room! How it would be discussed, how condemned, how deplored! Not one of the nurses of that little band but would not feel herself hurt by what she had done—by what she had been forced to do. And the news of her failure would spread to all her acquaintances and friends throughout the City. Dr. Street would know it; every physician to whom she had hitherto been so welcome an aid would know it. In all the hospitals it would be a nine days' gossip. Campbell would hear of it, and Hattie.

All at once, within thirty feet of the house, Lloyd turned about and walked rapidly away from it. The movement was all but involuntary; every instinct in her, every sense of shame, brusquely revolted. It was stronger than she. A power, for the moment irresistible, dragged her back from that doorway. Once entering here, she left all hope behind. Yet the threshold must be crossed, yet the hope must be abandoned.

She felt that if she faced about now a second time she would indeed attract attention. So, while her cheeks flamed hot at the meanness, the miserable ridiculousness of the imposture, she assumed a brisk, determined gait, as though she knew just where she were going, and, turning out of the square down a by-street, walked around the block, even stopping once or twice before a store, pretending an interest in the display. It seemed to her that by now everybody in the streets must have noted that there was something wrong with her. Twice as a passer-by brushed past her she looked back to see if he was watching her. How to live through the next ten minutes? If she were only in her room, bolted in, locked and double-locked in. Why was there not some back way through which she could creep to that seclusion?

And so it was that Lloyd came back to the house she had built, to the little community she had so proudly organised, to the agency she had founded, and with her own money endowed and supported.

At last she found herself at the bottom of the steps, her foot upon the lowest one, her hand clasping the heavy bronze rail. There was no going back now. She went up and pushed the button of the electric bell, and then, the step once taken, the irrevocable once dared, something like the calmness of resignation came to her. There was no help for it. Now for the ordeal. Rownie opened the door for her with a cheery welcome. Lloyd was dimly conscious that the girl said something about her mail, and that she was just in time for supper. But the hall and stairway were deserted and empty, while from the dining-room came a subdued murmur of conversation and the clink of dishes. The nurses were at supper, as Lloyd had hoped. The moment favoured her, and she brushed by Rownie, and almost ran, panic-stricken and trembling, up the stairs.

She gained the hall of the second floor. There was the door of her room standing ajar. With a little gasp of infinite relief, she hurried to it, entered, shut and locked and bolted it behind her, and, casting her satchel and handbag from her, flung herself down upon the great couch, and buried her head deep among the cushions.

At Lloyd's abrupt entrance Miss Douglass turned about from the book-shelves in an angle of the room and stared a moment in no little surprise. Then she exclaimed:

"Why, Lloyd, why, what is it—what is the matter?"

Lloyd sprang up sharply at the sound of her voice, and then sank down to a sitting posture upon the edge of the couch. Quietly enough she said:

"Oh, is it you? I didn't know—expect to find any one——"

"You don't mind, do you? I just ran in to get a book—something to read. I've had a headache all day, and didn't go down to supper."

Lloyd nodded. "Of course—I don't mind," she said, a little wearily.

"But tell me," continued the fever nurse, "whatever is the matter? When you came in just now—I never saw you so—oh, I understand, your case at Medford——"

Lloyd's hands closed tight upon the edge of the couch.

"No one could have got a patient through when the fever had got as far as that," continued the other. "This must have been the fifth or sixth week. The second telegram came just in time to prevent my going. I was just going out of the door when the boy came with it."

"You? What telegram?" inquired Lloyd.

"Yes, I was on call. The first despatch asking for another extra nurse came about two o'clock. The four-twenty was the first train I could have taken—the two-forty-five express is a through train and don't stop at Medford—and, as I say, I was just going out of the door when Dr. Pitts's second despatch came, countermanding the first, and telling us that the patient had died. It seems that it was one of the officers of the Freja expedition. We didn't know——"

"Died?" interrupted Lloyd, looking fixedly at her.

"But Lloyd, you mustn't take it so to heart. You couldn't have got him through. No one could at that time. He was probably dying when you were sent for. We must all lose a case now and then."

"Died?" repeated Lloyd; "Dr. Pitts wired that Mr. Ferriss died?"

"Yes; it was to prevent my coming out there uselessly. He must have sent the wire quite an hour before you left. It was very thoughtful of him."

"He's dead," said Lloyd in a low, expressionless voice, looking vacantly about the room. "Mr.

Ferriss is dead." Then suddenly she put a fist to
either temple, horror-struck and for the moment
shaken with hysteria from head to foot, her eyes
widening with an expression almost of terror.
" Dead!" she cried. " Oh, it's horrible! Why
didn't I—why couldn't I——"

" I know just how you feel," answered Miss
Douglass soothingly. " I am that way myself sometimes. It's not professional, I know, but when you
have been successful in two or three bad cases you
think you can always win; and then when you lose
the next case you believe that somehow it must
have been your fault—that if you had been a little
more careful at just that moment, or done a little
different in that particular point, you might have
saved your patient. But you, of all people, ought
not to feel like that. If you could not have saved
your case nobody could."

" It was just because I had the case that it was
lost."

" Nonsense, Lloyd; don't talk like that. You've
not had enough sleep; your nerves have been over-
strained. You're worn out and a little hysterical
and morbid. Now lie down and keep quiet, and I'll
bring you your supper. You need a good night's
sleep and bromide of potassium."

When she had gone Lloyd rose to her feet and
drew her hand wearily across her eyes. The situation adjusted itself in her mind. After the first
recoil of horror at Ferriss's death she was able to
see the false position in which she stood. She had
been so certain already that Ferriss would die, leaving him as she did at so critical a moment, that now

the sharpness of Miss Douglass's news was blunted a little. She had only been unprepared for the suddenness of the shock. But now she understood clearly how Miss Douglass had been deceived by circumstances. The fever nurse had heard of Ferriss's death early in the afternoon, and supposed, of course, that Lloyd had left the case *after*, and not before, it had occurred. This was the story the other nurses would believe. Instantly, in the flood of grief and remorse and humiliation that had overwhelmed her, Lloyd caught at this straw of hope. Only Dr. Pitts and Bennett knew the real facts. Bennett, of course, would not speak, and Lloyd knew that the physician would understand the cruelty and injustice of her situation, and because of that would also keep silence. To make sure of this she could write him a letter, or, better still, see him personally. It would be hard to tell him the truth. But that was nothing when compared with the world's denunciation of her.

If she had really been false to her charge, if she had actually flinched and faltered at the crucial moment, had truly been the coward, this deception which had been thrust upon her at the moment of her return to the house, this part which it was so easy to play, would have been a hideous and unspeakable hypocrisy. But Lloyd had not faltered, had not been false. In her heart of hearts she had been true to herself and to her trust. How would she deceive her companions then by allowing them to continue in the belief of her constancy, fidelity, and courage? What she hid from them, or rather what they could not see, was a state of things that it was impossible for any one but herself to understand. She could not—no woman could—bring herself to confess to another woman what had happened that day at Medford. It would be believed that she could have stayed at her patient's bedside if she had so desired. No one who did not know Bennett could understand the terrible, vast force of the man.

Try as she would, Lloyd could not but think first of herself at this moment. Bennett was ignored, forgotten. Once she had loved him, but that was all over now. The thought of Ferriss's death, for which in a manner she had been forced to be responsible, came rushing to her mind from time to time, and filled her with a horror and, at times, even a perverse sense of remorse, almost beyond words. But Lloyd's pride, her self-confidence, her strength of character and independence had been dearer to her than almost anything in life. So she told herself, and, at that moment, honestly believed. And though she knew that her pride had been humbled, it was not gone, and enough of it remained to make her desire and strive to keep the fact a secret from the world. It seemed very easy. She would only have to remain passive. Circumstances acted for her.

Miss Douglass returned, followed by Rownie carrying a tray. When the mulatto had gone, after arranging Lloyd's supper on a little table near the couch, the fever nurse drew up a chair.

" Now we can talk," she said, " unless you are too tired. I've been so interested in this case at Medford. Tell me what was the immediate cause of death ; was it perforation or just gradual collapse ? "

"It was neither," said Lloyd quickly. "It was a hæmorrhage."

She had uttered the words with as little consciousness as a phonograph, and the lie had escaped her before she was aware. How did she know what had been the immediate cause of death? What right had she to speak? Why was it that all at once a falsehood had come so easy to her, to her whose whole life until then had been so sincere, so genuine?

"A hæmorrhage?" repeated the other. "Had there been many before then? Was there coma vigil when the end came? I——"

"Oh," cried Lloyd with a quick gesture of impatience, "don't, don't ask me any more. I am tired—nervous; I am worn out."

"Yes, of course you must be," answered the fever nurse. "We won't talk any more about it."

That night and the following day were terrible. Lloyd neither ate nor slept. Not once did she set foot out of her room, giving out that she was ill, which was not far from the truth, and keeping to herself and to the companionship of the thoughts and terrors that crowded her mind. Until that day at Medford her life had run easily and happily and in well-ordered channels. She was successful in her chosen profession and work. She imagined herself to be stronger and of finer fibre than most other women, and her love for Bennett had lent a happiness and a sweetness to her life dear to her beyond all words. Suddenly, and within an hour's time, she had lost everything. Her will had been broken, her spirit crushed; she had been forced to become fearfully instrumental in causing the death of her patient—a man who loved and trusted her—while her love for Bennett, which for years had been her deep and abiding joy, the one great influence of her life, was cold and dead, and could never be revived.

This in the end came to be Lloyd's greatest grief. She could forget that she herself had been humbled and broken. Horrible, unspeakably horrible, as Ferriss's death seemed to her, it was upon Bennett, and not upon her, that its responsibility must be laid. She had done what she could. Of that she was assured. But, first and above all things, Lloyd was a woman, and her love for Bennett was a very different matter.

When, during that never-to-be-forgotten scene in the breakfast-room of the doctor's house, she had warned Bennett that if he persisted in his insane resolution he would stamp out her affection for him, Lloyd had only half believed what she said. But when at last it dawned upon her that she had spoken wiser than she knew, that this was actually true, and that now, no matter how she might desire it, she could not love him any longer, it seemed as though her heart must break. It was precisely as though Bennett himself, the Bennett she had known, had been blotted out of existence. It was much worse than if Bennett had merely died. Even then he would have still existed for her, somewhere. As it was, the man she had known simply ceased to be, irrevocably, finally, and the warmth of her love dwindled and grew cold, because now there was nothing left for it to feed upon.

Never until then had Lloyd realised how much

he had been to her; how he had not only played so
large a part in her life, but how he had become a
very part of her life itself. Her love for him had
been like the air, like the sunlight; was delicately
knitted and intertwined into all the innumerable
intricacies of her life and character. Literally, not
an hour had ever passed that, directly or indirectly,
he had not occupied her thoughts. He had been
her inspiration; he had made her want to be brave
and strong and determined, and it was because of
him that the greater things of the world interested
her. She had chosen a work to be done because
he had set her an example. So only that she preserved her womanliness, she, too, wanted to count,
to help on, to have her place in the world's progress.
In reality all her ambitions and hopes had been
looking toward one end only, that she might be
his equal; that he might find in her a companion
and a confidante; one who could share his enthu-
siasms and understand his vast projects and great
aims.

And how had he treated her when at last opportunity had been given her to play her part, to be
courageous and strong, to prevail against great
odds, while he stood by to see? He had ignored
and misunderstood, and tossed aside as childish and
absurd that which she had been building up for
years. Instead of appreciating her heroism he had
forced her to become a coward in the eyes of the
world. She had hoped to be his equal, and he had
treated her as a school-girl. It had all been a mistake. She was not and could not be the woman
she had hoped. He was not and never had been

the man she had imagined. They had nothing in common.

But it was not easy to give Bennett up, to let him pass out of her life. She wanted to love him yet. With all her heart and strength, in spite of everything—woman that she was, she had come to that— in spite of everything she wanted to love him. Though he had broken her will, thwarted her ambitions, ignored her cherished hopes, misunderstood and mistaken her, yet, if she could, Lloyd would yet have loved him, loved him even for the very fact that he had been stronger than she.

Again and again she tried to awaken this dead affection, to call back this vanished love. She tried to remember the Bennett she had known; she told herself that he loved her; that he had said that the great things he had done had been done only with an eye to her approval; that she had been his inspiration no less than he had been hers; that he had fought his way back, not only to life, but to her. She thought of all he had suffered, of the hardships and privations beyond her imagination to conceive, that he had undergone. She tried to recall the infinite joy of that night when the news of his safe return had come to her; she thought of him at his very best—how he had always seemed to her the type of the perfect man, masterful, aggressive, accomplishing great projects with an energy and determination almost superhuman, one of the world's great men, whose name the world still shouted. She called to mind how the very ruggedness of his face, with its massive lines and harsh angles, had attracted her; how she had been proud of his giant's

strength, the vast span of his shoulders, the bull-
like depth of his chest, the sense of enormous physical power suggested by his every movement.

But it was all of no effect. That Bennett was
worse than dead to her. The Bennett that now
came to her mind and imagination was the brutal,
perverse man of the breakfast-room at Medford,
coarse, insolent, intractable, stamping out all that
was finest in her, breaking and flinging away the
very gifts he had inspired her to offer him. It was
nothing to him that she should stand degraded in
the eyes of the world. He did not want her to be
brave and strong. She had been wrong; it was not
that kind of woman he desired. He had not ac-
knowledged that she, too, as well as he—a woman
as well as a man might have her principles, her
standards of honour, her ideas of duty. It was not
her character, then, that he prized; the nobility of her
nature was nothing to him; he took no thought of
the fine-wrought texture of her mind. How, then,
did she appeal to him? It was not her mind; it
was not her soul. What, then, was left? Nothing
but the physical. The shame of it; the degradation
of it! To be so cruelly mistaken in the man she
loved, to be able to appeal to him only on his lower
side! Lloyd clasped her hands over her eyes, shutting her teeth hard against a cry of grief and pain
and impotent anger. No, no, now it was irrevocable; now her eyes were opened. The Bennett she
had known and loved had been merely a creature
of her own imagining; the real man had suddenly
discovered himself; and this man, in spite of herself,
she hated as a victim hates its tyrant.

But her grief for her vanished happiness—the happiness that this love, however mistaken, had brought into her life—was pitiful. Lloyd could not think of it without the choke coming to her throat and the tears brimming her dull-blue eyes, while at times a veritable paroxysm of sorrow seized upon her and flung her at full length upon her couch, her face buried and her whole body shaken with stifled sobs. It was gone, it was gone, and could never be called back. What was there now left to her to live for? Why continue her profession? Why go on with the work? What pleasure now in striving and overcoming? Where now was the exhilaration of battle with the Enemy, even supposing she yet had the strength to continue the fight? Who was there now to please, to approve, to encourage? To what end the days of grave responsibilities, the long, still nights of vigil?

She began to doubt herself. Bennett, the man, had loved his work for its own sake. But how about herself, the woman? In what spirit had she gone about her work? Had she been genuine, after all? Had she not undertaken it rather as a means than as an end—not because she cared for it, but because she thought he would approve, because she had hoped by means of the work she would come into closer companionship with him? She wondered if this must always be so—the man loving the work for the work's sake; the woman, more complex, weaker, and more dependent, doing the work only in reference to the man.

But often she distrusted her own conclusions, and, no doubt, rightly so. Her mind was yet too confused to reason calmly, soberly, and accurately. Her distress was yet too keen, too poignant to permit her to be logical. At one time she was almost ready to admit that she had misjudged Bennett; that, though he had acted cruelly and unjustly, he had done what he thought was best. His sacrifice of Ferriss was sufficient guarantee of his sincerity. But this mistrust of herself did not affect her feeling toward him. There were moments when she condoned his offence; there was never an instant she did not hate him.

And this sentiment of hatred itself, independent of and apart from its object, was distasteful and foreign to her. Never in her life had Lloyd hated any one before. To be kind, to be gentle, to be womanly was her second nature, and kindness, gentleness, and womanliness were qualities that her profession only intensified and deepened. This newcomer in her heart, this fierce, evil visitor, that goaded her and pricked and harried her from day to day and throughout so many waking nights, that roused the unwonted flash in her eye and drove the hot, angry blood to her smooth, white forehead and knotted her levelled brows to a dark and lowering frown, had entered her life and being, unsought for and undesired. It did not belong to her world. Yet there it sat on its usurped throne deformed and hideous, driving out all tenderness and compunction, ruling her with a rod of iron, hardening her, embittering her, and belittling her, making a mockery of all sweetness, fleering at nobility and magnanimity, lowering the queen to the level of the fishwife.

A Man's Woman

When the first shock of the catastrophe had spent its strength and Lloyd perforce must turn again to the life she had to live, groping for its scattered, tangled ends, piecing together again as best she might its broken fragments, she set herself honestly to drive this hatred from her heart. If she could not love Bennett, at least she need not hate him. She was moved to this by no feeling of concern for Bennett. It was not a consideration that she owed to him, but something rather that was due to herself. Yet, try as she would, the hatred still remained. She could not put it from her. Hurt her and contaminate her as it did, in spite of all her best efforts, in spite of her very prayers, the evil thing abode with her, deep-rooted, strong, malignant. She saw that in the end she would continue in her profession, but she believed that she could not go on with it consistently, based as it was upon sympathy and love and kindness, while a firm-seated, active hatred dwelt with her, harassing her at every moment, and perverting each good impulse and each unselfish desire. It was an ally of the very Enemy she would be called upon to fight, a traitor that at any moment might open the gates to his triumphant entry.

But was this his only ally; was this the only false and ugly invader that had taken advantage of her shattered defence? Had the unwelcome visitor entered her heart alone? Was there not a companion still more wicked, more perverted, more insidious, more dangerous? For the first time Lloyd knew what it meant to deceive.

It was supposed by her companions, and accepted

by them as a matter of course, that she had not left
the bedside of her patient until after his death. At
first she had joyfully welcomed this mistake as her
salvation, the one happy coincidence that was to
make her life possible, and for a time had ceased to
think about it. That phase of the incident was
closed. Matters would readjust themselves. In a
few days' time the incident would be forgotten. But
she found that she herself could not forget it, and
that as days went on the idea of this passive, silent
deception she was obliged to maintain occurred to
her oftener and oftener. She remembered again
how glibly and easily she had lied to her friend upon
the evening of her return. How was it that the lie
had flowed so smoothly from her lips? To her
knowledge she had never deliberately lied before.
She would have supposed that, because of this fact,
falsehood would come difficult to her, that she would
have bungled, hesitated, stammered. But it was the
reverse that had been the case. The facility with
which she had uttered the lie was what now began to
disturb and to alarm her. It argued some sudden
collapse of her whole system of morals, some fundamental disarrangement of the entire machine.

Abruptly she recoiled. Whither was she tending? If she supinely resigned herself to the current
of circumstance, where would she be carried? Yet
how was she to free herself from the current, how to
face this new situation that suddenly presented itself
at a time when she had fancied the real shock of
battle and contention was spent and past?

How was she to go back now? How could she
retrace her steps? There was but one way—cor-

rect the false impression. It would not be necessary to acknowledge that she had been forced to
leave her post; the essential was that her companions should know that she had deceived them—that
she had left the bedside *before* her patient's death.
But at the thought of making such confession, public as it must be, everything that was left of her
wounded pride revolted. She who had been so firm,
she who had held so tenaciously to her principles,
she who had posed before them as an example of
devotion and courage—she could not bring herself
to that.

" No, no," she exclaimed as this alternative presented itself to her mind. " No, I cannot. It is
beyond me. I simply cannot do it."

But she could. Yes, she could do it if she would.
Deep down in her mind that little thought arose.
She could if she wanted to. Hide it though she
might, cover it and bury it with what false reasoning
she could invent, the little thought would not be
smothered, would not be crushed out. Well, then,
she would not. Was it not her chance; was not
this deception which others and not herself had
created, her opportunity to recover herself, to live
down what had been done—what she had been
forced to do, rather? Absolute right was never to
be attained; was not life to be considered rather in
the light of a compromise between good and evil?
To do what one could under the circumstances, was
not that the golden mean?

But she ought. And, quick, another little thought
sprang up in the deeper recesses of her mind and
took its place beside the other. It was right that

she should be true. She ought to do the right. Argument, the pleas of weakness, the demands of expediency, the plausibility of compromise were all of no avail. The idea " I ought " persisted and persisted and persisted. She could and she ought. There was no excuse for her, and no sooner had she thrust aside the shifty mass of sophistries under which she had striven to conceal them, no sooner had she let in the light, than these two conceptions of Duty and Will began suddenly to grow.

But what was she to gain? What would be the result of such a course as her conscience demanded she should adopt? It was inevitable that she would be misunderstood, cruelly misjudged. What action would her confession entail? She could not say. But results did not matter; what she was to gain or lose did not matter. Around her and before her all was dark and vague and terrible. If she was to escape there was but one thing to do. Suddenly her own words came back to her:

" All we can do is to hold to what we know is right, and trust that everything will come well in the end."

She knew what was right, and she had the strength to hold to it. Then all at once there came to Lloyd a grand, breathless sense of uplifting, almost a transfiguration. She felt herself carried high above the sphere of little things, the region of petty considerations. What did she care for consequences, what mattered to her the unjust condemnation of her world, if only she remained true to herself, if only she did right? What did she care for what she gained? It was no longer a question of gain or loss—it was a question of being true and strong and brave. The conflict of that day at Medford between the man's power and the woman's resistance had been cruel, the crisis had been intense, and though she had been conquered then, had it, after all, been beyond recall? No, she was not conquered. No, she was not subdued. Her will had not been broken, her courage had not been daunted, her strength had not been weakened. Here was the greater fight, here was the higher test. Here was the ultimate, supreme crisis of all, and here, at last, come what might, she would not, would not, would not fail.

As soon as Lloyd reached this conclusion she sat about carrying her resolution into effect.

"If I don't do it now while I'm strong," she told herself, "if I wait, I never will do it."

Perhaps there was yet a touch of the hysterical in her actions even then. The jangled feminine nerves were yet vibrating far above their normal pitch; she was overwrought and oversensitive, for just as a fanatic rushes eagerly upon the fire and the steel, preferring the more exquisite torture, so Lloyd sought out the more painful situation, the more trying ordeal, the line of action that called for the greatest fortitude, the most unflinching courage.

She chose to make known her real position, to correct the false impression at a time when all the nurses of the house should be together. This would be at supper-time. Since her return from Medford, Lloyd had shut herself away from the other inmates of the house, and had taken her meals

in her room. With the exception of Miss Douglass
and the superintendent nurse no one had seen her.
She had passed her time lying at full length upon
her couch, her hands clasped behind her head, or
pacing the floor, or gazing listlessly out of her windows, while her thoughts raced at a gallop through
her mind.

Now, however, she bestirred herself. She had
arrived at her final decision early in the afternoon
of the third day after her return, and at once she
resolved that she would endure the ordeal that very
evening.

She passed the intervening time, singularly
enough, in very carefully setting her room to rights,
adjusting and readjusting the few ornaments on
the mantel-shelf and walls, winding the clock that
struck ship's bells instead of the hours, and minutely
sorting the letters and papers in her desk. It was
the same as if she were going upon a long journey
or were preparing for a great sickness. Toward
four o'clock Miss Douglass, looking in to ask how
she did, found her before her mirror carefully comb-
ing and arranging her great bands and braids of
dark-red hair. The fever nurse declared that she
was immensely improved in appearance, and asked
at once if she was not feeling better.

"Yes," answered Lloyd, "very much better,"
adding: "I shall be down to supper to-night."

For some reason that she could not explain
Lloyd took unusual pains with her toilet, debating
long over each detail of dress and ornament. At
length, toward five o'clock, she was ready, and sat
down by her window, a book in her lap, to await

the announcement of supper as the condemned
await the summons to execution.

Her plan was to delay her appearance in the
dining-room until she was sure that everybody was
present; then she would go down, and, standing
there before them all, say what she had to say, state
the few bald facts of the case, without excuse or
palliation, and leave them to draw the one inevitable
conclusion.

But this final hour of waiting was a long agony
for Lloyd. Her moods changed with every moment; the action she contemplated presented itself
to her mind in a multitude of varying lights. At
one time she quivered with the apprehension of it,
as though at the slow approach of hot irons. At
another she could see no reason for being greatly
concerned over the matter. Did the whole affair
amount to so much, after all? Her companions
would, of their own accord, make excuses for her.
Risking one's life in the case of a virulent, con-
tagious disease was no small matter. No one could
be blamed for leaving such a case. At one moment
Lloyd's idea of public confession seemed to her little
less than sublime; at another, almost ridiculous.
But she remembered the case of Harriet Freeze,
who had been unable to resist the quiet, unexpressed
force of opinion of her fellow-workers. It would
be strange if Lloyd should find herself driven from
the very house she had built.

The hour before supper-time seemed interminable; the quarter passed, then the half, then the three-
quarters. Lloyd imagined she began to detect a
faint odour of the kitchen in the air. Suddenly the

remaining minutes of the hour began to be stricken
from the dial of her clock with bewildering rapidity.
From the drawing-room immediately below came
the sounds of the piano. That was Esther Thielman, no doubt, playing one of her interminable
Polish compositions. All at once the piano stopped,
and, with a quick sinking of the heart, Lloyd heard
the sliding doors separating the drawing-room from
the dining-room roll back. Miss Douglass and
another one of the nurses, Miss Truslow, a young
girl, a newcomer in the house, came out of the
former's room and went downstairs, discussing the
merits of burlap as preferable to wall-paper. Lloyd
even heard Miss Truslow remark:

" Yes, that's very true, but if it isn't sized it will
wrinkle in damp weather."

Rownie came to Lloyd's door and knocked, and,
without waiting for a reply, said:

" Dinneh's served, Miss Searight," and Lloyd
heard her make the same announcement at Miss
Bergyn's room farther down the hall. One by one
Lloyd heard the others go downstairs. The rooms
and hallways on the second floor fell quiet. A faint,
subdued murmur of talk came to her ears in the
direction of the dining-room. Lloyd waited for
five, for ten, for fifteen minutes. Then she rose,
drawing in her breath, straightening herself to her
full height. She went to the door, then paused for
a moment, looking back at all the familiar objects—
the plain, rich furniture, the book-shelves, the great,
comfortable couch, the old-fashioned round mirror
that hung between the windows, and her writing-
desk of blackened mahogany. It seemed to her

that in some way she was never to see these things again, as if she were saying good-bye to them and to the life she had led in that room and in their surroundings. She would be a different woman when she came back to that room. Slowly she descended the stairs and halted for a moment in the hall below. It was not too late to turn back even now. She could hear her companions at their supper very plainly, and could distinguish Esther Thielman's laugh as she exclaimed:

"Why, of course, that's the very thing I mean."

It was a strange surprise that Lloyd had in store for them all. Her heart began to beat heavy and thick. Could she even find her voice to speak when the time came? Would it not be better to put it off, to think over the whole matter again between now and to-morrow morning? But she moved her head impatiently. No, she would not turn back. She found that the sliding doors in the drawing-room had been closed, and so went to the door that opened into the dining-room from the hall itself. It stood ajar. Lloyd pushed it open, entered, and, closing the door behind her, stood there leaning against it.

The table was almost full; only two or three places besides her own were unoccupied. There was Miss Bergyn at the head; the fever nurse, Miss Douglass, at her right, and, lower down, Lloyd saw Esther Thielman; Delia Craig, just back from a surgical case of Dr. Street's; Miss Page, the oldest and most experienced nurse of them all; Gilbertson, whom every one called by her last name; Miss Ives and

Eleanor Bogart, who had both taken doctors' degrees, and could have practised if they had desired; Miss Wentworth, who had served an apprenticeship in a missionary hospital in Armenia, and had known Clara Barton, and, last of all, the newcomer, Miss Truslow, very young and very pretty, who had never yet had a case, and upon whose diploma the ink was hardly dry.

At first, so quietly had she entered, no one took any notice of Lloyd, and she stood a moment, her back to the door, wondering how she should begin. Everybody seemed to be in the best of humour; a babel of talk was in the air; conversations were going forward, carried on across the table, or over intervening shoulders.

" Why, of course, don't you see, that's the very thing I meant——"

"——I think you can get that already sized, though, and with a stencil figure if you want it——"

" ——Really, it's very interesting; the first part is stupid, but she has some very good ideas."

"——Yes, at Vanoni's. But we get a reduction, you know——"

"——and, oh, listen; this is too funny; she turned around and said, very prim and stiff, ' No, indeed; I'm too old a woman.' Funny! If I think of that on my deathbed I shall laugh——"

"——and so that settled it. How could I go on after that——? "

"——Must you tack it on? The walls are so hard——"

" Let Rownie do it; she knows. Oh, here's the invalid! "

"Oh, why, it's Lloyd! We're so glad you're able to come down!"

But when they had done exclaiming over her reappearance among them Lloyd still remained as she was, her back against the door, standing very straight, her hands at her side. She did not immediately reply. Heads were turned in her direction. The talk fell away by rapid degrees as they began to notice the paleness of her face and the strange, firm set of her mouth.

"Sit down, Lloyd," said Miss Bergyn; "don't stand. You are not very well yet; I'll have Rownie bring you a glass of sherry."

There was a silence. Then at length:

"No," said Lloyd quietly. "I don't want any sherry. I don't want any supper. I came down to tell you that you are all wrong in thinking I did what I could with my typhoid case at Medford. You think I left only after the patient had died. I did not; I left before. There was a crisis of some kind. I don't know what it was, because I was not in the sick-room at the time, and I did not go when I was called. The doctor was not there either; he had gone out and left the case in my charge. There was nobody with the patient but a servant. The servant called me, but I did not go. Instead I came away and left the house. The patient died that same day. It is that that I wanted to tell you. Do you all understand—perfectly? . I left my patient at the moment of a crisis, and with no one with him but a servant. And he died that same afternoon."

Then she went out, and the closing of the door

jarred sharply upon the great silence that had spread throughout the room.

Lloyd went back to her room, closed and locked the door, and, sinking down upon the floor by the couch, bowed her head upon her folded arms. But she was in no mood for weeping, and her eyes were dry. She was conscious chiefly that she had taken an irrevocable step, that her head had begun to ache. There was no exhilaration in her mind now; she did not feel any of the satisfaction of attainment after struggle, of triumph after victory. More than once she even questioned herself if, after all, her confession had been necessary. But now she was weary unto death of the whole wretched business. Now she only knew that her head was aching fiercely; she did not care either to look into the past or forward into the future. The present occupied her; for the present her head was aching.

But before Lloyd went to bed that night Miss Bergyn knew the whole truth as to what had happened at Dr. Pitts's house. The superintendent nurse had followed Lloyd to her room almost immediately, and would not be denied. She knew very well that Lloyd Searight had never left a dying patient of her own volition. Intuitively she guessed at something hidden.

"Lloyd," she said decisively, "don't ask me to believe that you went of your own free will. Tell me just what happened. Why did you go? Ask me to believe anything but that you—no, I won't say the word. There was some very good reason, wasn't there?"

"I—I cannot explain," Lloyd answered. "You

must think what you choose. You wouldn't understand."

But, happily, when Lloyd's reticence finally broke Miss Bergyn did understand. The superintendent nurse knew Bennett only by report. But Lloyd she had known for years, and realised that if she had yielded, it had only been after the last hope had been tried. In the end Lloyd told her everything that had occurred. But, though she even admitted Bennett's affection for her, she said nothing about herself, and Miss Bergyn did not ask.

"I know, of course," said the superintendent nurse at length, "you hate to think that you were made to go; but men are stronger than women, Lloyd, and such a man as that must be stronger than most men. You were not to blame because you left the case, and you are certainly not to blame for Mr. Ferriss's death. Now I shall give it out here in the house that you had a very good reason for leaving your case, and that while we can't explain it any more particularly, I have had a talk with you and know all about it, and am perfectly satisfied. Then I shall go out to Medford and see Dr. Pitts. It would be best," she added, for Lloyd had made a gesture of feeble dissent. "He must understand perfectly, and we need not be afraid of any talk about the matter at all. What has happened has happened ' in the profession,' and I don't believe it will go any further."

.   .   .   .

Lloyd returned to Bannister toward the end of the week. How long she would remain she did not know, but for the present the association of the other nurses was more than she was able to bear. Later, when the affair had become something of an old story, she would return, resuming her work as though nothing had happened.

Hattie met her at the railway station with the phaëton and the ponies. She was radiant with delight at the prospect of having Lloyd all to herself for an indefinite period of time.

"And you didn't get sick, after all?" she exclaimed, clasping her hands. "Was your patient as sick as I was? Weren't his parents glad that you made him well again?"

Lloyd put her hand over the little girl's mouth.

"Let us not talk any 'shop,' Hattie," she said, trying to smile.

But on the morning after her arrival Lloyd woke in her own white room of the old farm-house, abruptly conscious of some subtle change that had occurred to her overnight. For the first time since the scene in the breakfast-room at Medford she was aware of a certain calmness that had come to her. Perhaps she had at last begun to feel the good effects of the trial by fire which she had voluntarily undergone—to know a certain happiness that now there was no longer any deceit in her heart. This she had uprooted and driven out by force of her own will. It was gone. But now, on this morning, she seemed to feel that this was not all.

Something else had left her—something that of late had harassed her and goaded her and embittered her life, and mocked at her gentleness and kindness, was gone. That fierce, truculent hatred that she had so striven to put from her, now behold!

of its own accord, it had seemed to leave her. How had it happened? Before she had dared the ordeal of confession this feeling of hatred, this perverse and ugly changeling that had brooded in her heart, had seemed too strong, too deeply seated to be moved. Now, suddenly, it had departed, unbidden, without effort on her part.

Vaguely Lloyd wondered at this thing. In driving deceit from her it would appear that she had also driven out hatred, that the one could not stay so soon as the other had departed. Could the one exist apart from the other? Was there, then, some strange affinity in all evil, as, perhaps, in all good, so that a victory over one bad impulse meant a victory over many? Without thought of gain or of reward, she had held to what was right through the confusion and storm and darkness. Was this to be, after all, her reward, her gain? Possibly; but she could not tell, she could not see. The confusion was subsiding, the storm had passed, but much of the darkness yet remained. Deceit she had fought from out her heart; silently Hatred had stolen after it. Love had not returned to his old place, and never, never would, but the changeling was gone, and the house was swept and garnished.

VIII.

The day after the funeral, Bennett returned alone to Dr. Pitts's house at Medford, and the same evening his trunks and baggage, containing his papers —the records, observations, journals, and log-books of the expedition—followed him.

As Bennett entered the gate of the place that he had chosen to be his home for the next year, he was aware that the windows of one of the front rooms upon the second floor were wide open, the curtains tied up into loose knots; inside a servant came and went, putting the room to rights again, airing it and changing the furniture. In the road before the house he had seen the marks of the wheels of the undertaker's wagon where it had been backed up to the horse-block. As he closed the front door behind him and stood for a moment in the hallway, his valise in his hand, he saw, hanging upon one of the pegs of the hat-rack, the hat Ferriss had last worn. Bennett put down his valise quickly, and, steadying himself against the wall, leaned heavily against it, drawing a deep breath, his eyes closing.

The house was empty and, but for the occasional subdued noises that came from the front room at the end of the hall, silent. Bennett picked up his valise again and went upstairs to the rooms that had been set apart for him. He did not hang his hat upon the hat-rack, but carried it with him.

A Man's Woman

The housekeeper, who met him at the head of the
stairs and showed him the way to his apartments,
inquired of him as to the hours he wished to have
his meals served. Bennett told her, and then added:
"I will have all my meals in the breakfast-room,
the one you call the glass-room, I believe. And as
soon as the front room is ready I shall sleep there.
That will be my room after this."

The housekeeper stared. "It won't be quite
safe, sir, for some time. The doctor gave very strict
orders about ventilating it and changing the furniture."

Bennett merely nodded as if to say he understood,
and the housekeeper soon after left him to himself. The afternoon passed, then the evening. Such
supper as Bennett could eat was served according
to his orders in the breakfast-room. Afterward he
called Kamiska, and went for a long walk over the
country roads in a direction away from the town,
proceeding slowly, his hands clasped behind his
back. Later, toward ten o'clock, he returned. He
went upstairs toward his room with the half-formed
idea of looking over and arranging his papers before going to bed. Sleep he could not; he foresaw
that clearly.

But Bennett was not yet familiar with the ar-
rangement of the house. His mind was busy with
other things; he was thoughtful, abstracted, and
upon reaching the stair landing on the second floor,
turned toward the front of the house when he should
have turned toward the rear. He entered what he
supposed to be his room, lit the gas, then stared
about him in some perplexity.

A Man's Woman

The room he was in was almost bare of furniture. Even part of the carpet had been taken up. The windows were wide open; a stale odour of drugs pervaded the air, while upon the bed nothing remained but the mattress and bolster. For a moment Bennett looked about him bewildered, then he started sharply. This was—had been—the sick-room. Here, upon that bed, Ferriss had died; here had been enacted one scene in the terrible drama wherein he, Bennett, had played so conspicuous a part.

As Bennett stood there looking about him, one hand upon the footboard of the bed, a strange, formless oppression of the spirit weighed heavily upon him. He seemed to see upon that naked bed the wasted, fever-stricken body of the dearest friend he had ever known. It was as though Ferriss were lying in state there, with black draperies hung about the bier and candles burning at the head and foot. Death had been in that room. Empty though it was, a certain religious solemnity, almost a certain awe, seemed to bear down upon the senses. Before he knew it Bennett found himself kneeling at the denuded bed, his face buried, his arms flung wide across the place where Ferriss had last reposed.

He could not say how long he remained thus— perhaps ten minutes, perhaps an hour. He seemed to come to himself once more when he stepped out into the hall again, closing and locking the door of the death-room behind him. But now all thought of work had left him. In the morning he would arrange his papers. It was out of the question to think of sleep. He descended once more to the lower floor of the silent house, and stepped out again into the open air.

On the veranda, close beside him, was a deep-seated wicker arm-chair. Bennett sank down into it, drawing his hands wearily across his forehead. The stillness of a summer night had settled broadly over the vast, dim landscape. There was no moon; all the stars were out. Very far off a whippoorwill was calling incessantly. Once or twice from the little orchard close at hand an apple dropped with a faint rustle of leaves and a muffled, velvety impact upon the turf. Kamiska, wide awake, sat motionless upon her haunches on the steps, looking off into the night, cocking an ear to every faintest sound.

Well, Ferriss was dead, and he, Bennett, was responsible. His friend, the man whom most he loved, was dead. The splendid fight he had made for his life during that ferocious struggle with the Ice had been all of no effect. Without a murmur, without one complaint he had borne starvation, the bitter arctic cold, privation beyond words, the torture of the frost that had gnawed away his hands, the blinding fury of the snow and wind, the unceasing and incredible toil with sledge and pack—all the terrible hardship of an unsuccessful attempt to reach the Pole, only to die miserably in his bed, alone, abandoned by the man and woman whom, of all people of the world, he had most loved and trusted. And he, Bennett, had been to blame.

Was Ferriss conscious during that last moment? Did he know; would he, sometime, somewhere, know? It could not be said. Forever that must remain a mystery. And, after all, had Bennett done

right in keeping Lloyd from the sick-room? Now
that all was over, now that the whole fearful tragedy
could be judged somewhat calmly and in the light
of reason, the little stealthy doubt began to insinuate
itself.

At first he had turned from it, raging and furious,
stamping upon it as upon an intruding reptile. The
rough-hewn, simple-natured man, with his arrogant
and vast self-confidence, his blind, unshaken belief
in the wisdom of his own decisions, had never in his
life before been willing to admit that he could be
mistaken, that it was possible for him to resolve
upon a false line of action. He had always been
right. But now a change had come. A woman
had entangled herself in the workings of his world,
the world that hitherto had been only a world of
men for him—and now he faltered, now he questioned himself, now he scrutinised his motives, now
the simple became complicated, the straight
crooked, right mingled with wrong, bitter with
sweet, falseness with truth.

He who had faith in himself to remove mountains,
he who could drive his fellow-men as a herder drives
his sheep, he who had forced the vast grip of the
Ice, had, with a battering ram's force, crushed his
way through those terrible walls, shattered and
breached and broken down the barriers, now in
this situation involving a woman—had he failed?
Had he weakened? And bigger, stronger, and
more persistently doubt intruded itself into his mind.

Hitherto Bennett's only salvation from absolute
despair had been the firm consciousness of his own
rectitude. In that lay his only comfort, his only hope,

his one, strong-built fabric of defence. If that was undermined, if that was eaten away, what was there left for him? Carefully, painfully, and with such minuteness as he could command, he went over the whole affair from beginning to end, forcing his unwilling mind—so unaccustomed to such work—to weigh each chance, to gauge each opportunity. If *this* were so, if *that* had been done, then would *such* results have followed? Suppose he had not interfered, suppose he had stood aside, would Lloyd have run such danger, after all, and would Ferriss at this time have been alive, and perhaps recovering? Had he, Bennett, been absolutely mad; had he been blind and deaf to reason; had he acted the part of a brute —a purblind, stupid, and unutterably selfish brute— thinking chiefly of himself, after all, crushing the woman who was so dear to him, sacrificing the life of the man he loved, blundering in there, besotted and ignorant, acting the bully's part, unnecessarily frightened, cowardly where he imagined himself brave; weak, contemptibly weak, where he imagined himself strong? Might it not have been avoided if he had been even merely reasonable, as, in like case, an ordinary man would have been? He, who prided himself upon the promptness and soundness of his judgment in great crises, had lost his head and all power of self-control in this greatest crisis of all.

The doubt came back to him again and again. Trample it, stifle it, dash it from him as he would, each time it returned a little stronger, a little larger, a little more insistent. Perhaps, after all, he had made a mistake; perhaps, after all, Lloyd ran no great danger; perhaps, after all, Ferriss might now have been alive. All at once Bennett seemed to be sure of this.

Then it became terrible. Alone there, in the darkness and in the night, Bennett went down into the pit. Abruptly he seemed to come to himself—to realise what he had done, as if rousing from a nightmare. Remorse, horror, self-reproach, the anguish of bereavement, the infinite regret of things that never were to be again, the bitterness of a vanished love, self-contempt too abject for expression, the heart-breaking grief of the dreadful might-have-been, one by one, he knew them all. One by one, like the slow accumulation of gigantic burdens, the consequences of his folly descended upon him, heavier, more intolerably, more inexorably fixed with every succeeding moment, while the light of truth and reason searched every corner of his mind, and his doubt grew and hardened into certainty.

If only Bennett could have believed that, in spite of what had happened, Lloyd yet loved him, he could have found some ray of light in the darkness wherein he groped, some saving strength to bear the weight of his remorse and sorrow. But now, just in proportion as he saw clearer and truer he saw that he must look for no help in that direction. Being what Lloyd was, it was impossible for her, even though she wished it, to love him now—love the man who had broken her! The thought was preposterous. He remembered clearly that she had warned him of just this. No, that, too, the one sweetness of his rugged life, he must put from him as well—had already, and of his own accord, put from him.

How go on? Of what use now was ambition, endeavour, and the striving to attain great ends? The thread of his life was snapped; his friend was dead, and the love of the one woman of his world. For both he was to blame. Of what avail was it now to continue his work?

Ferriss was dead. Who now would stand at his side when the darkness thickened on ahead and obstacles drew across the path and Death overhead hung poised and menacing?

Lloyd's love for him was dead. Who now to bid him godspeed as his vessel's prow swung northward and the water whitened in her wake? Who now to wait behind when the great fight was dared again, to wait behind and watch for his home-coming; and when the mighty hope had been achieved, the goal of all the centuries attained, who now to send that first and dearest welcome out to him when the returning ship showed over the horizon's rim, flagged from her decks to her crosstrees in all the royal blazonry of an immortal triumph?

Now, that triumph was never to be for him. Ambition, too, was dead; some other was to win where now he could but lose, to gain where now he could but fail; some other stronger than he, more resolute, more determined. At last Bennett had come to this, he who once had been so imperial in the consciousness of his power, so arrogant, so uncompromising. Beaten, beaten at last; defeated, daunted, driven from his highest hopes, abandoning his dearest ambitions. And how, and why? Not by the Enemy he had so often faced and dared, not by any power external to himself; but by his very self's self, crushed by the engine he himself had set in motion, shattered by the recoil of the very force that for so long had dwelt within himself. Nothing in all the world could have broken him but that. Danger, however great, could not have cowed him; circumstances, however hopeless, could not have made him despair; obstacles, however vast, could not have turned him back. Himself was the only Enemy that could have conquered; his own power the only one to which he would have yielded. And fate had so ordered it that this one Enemy of all others, this one power of all others, had turned upon and rent him. The mystery of it! The terror of it! Why had he never known? How was it he had never guessed? What was this ruthless monster, this other self, that for so long had slept within his flesh, strong with his better strength, feeding and growing big with that he fancied was the best in him, that tricked him with his noblest emotion—the love of a good woman—lured him to a moment of weakness, then suddenly, and without warning, leaped at his throat and struck him to the ground?

He had committed one of those offences which the law does not reach, but whose punishment is greater than any law can inflict. Retribution had been fearfully swift. His career, Ferriss, and Lloyd—ambition, friendship, and the love of a woman—had been a trinity of dominant impulses in his life. Abruptly, almost in a single instant, he had lost them all, had thrown them away. He could never get them back. Bennett started sharply. What was this on his cheek; what was this that suddenly dimmed his eyes? Had it actually come to this? And this was he—Bennett—the same man who had commanded the Freja expedition. No, it was not the same man. That man was dead. He ground his teeth, shaken with the violence of emotions that seemed to be tearing his heart to pieces. Lost, lost to him forever! Bennett bowed his head upon his folded arms. Through his clenched teeth his words seemed almost wrenched from him, each word an agony.

"Dick—Dick, old man, you're gone, gone from me, and it was I who did it; and Lloyd, she too—she—God help me!"

Then the tension snapped. The great, massive frame shook with grief from head to heel, and the harsh, angular face, with its salient jaw and hard, uncouth lines, was wet with the first tears he had ever known.

He was roused at length by a sudden movement on the part of the dog. Kamiska had risen to her feet with a low growl, then, as the gate-latch clinked, she threw up her head and gave tongue to the night with all the force of her lungs. Bennett straightened up, thanking fortune that the night was dark, and looked about him. A figure was coming up the front walk, the gravel crunching under foot. It was the figure of a man. At the foot of the steps of the veranda he paused, and as Bennett made a movement turned in his direction and said:

"Is this Dr. Pitts's house?"

Bennett's reply was drowned in the clamour of the dog, but the other seemed to understand, for he answered:

A Man's Woman

" I'm looking for Mr. Ferriss—Richard Ferriss, of the Freja; they told me he was brought here."

Kamiska stopped her barking, sniffed once or twice at the man's trouser legs; then, in brusque frenzy of delight, leaped against him, licking his hands, dancing about him on two legs, whining and yelping.

Bennett came forward, and the man changed his position so that the light from the half-open front door shone upon his face.

" Why, Adler! " exclaimed Bennett; " well, where did you come from? "

" Mr. Bennett! " almost shouted the other, snatching off his cap. " It ain't really you, sir! " His face beamed and radiated a joy little short of beatitude. The man was actually trembling with happiness. Words failed him, and as with a certain clumsy tenderness he clasped Bennett's hand in both his own his old-time chief saw the tears in his eyes.

" Oh! Maybe I ain't glad to see you, sir—I thought you had gone away—I didn't know where —I—I didn't know as I was ever going to see you again."

Kamiska herself had been no less tremulously glad to see Adler than was Adler to see Bennett. He stammered, he confused himself, he shifted his weight from one foot to the other, his eyes danced, he laughed and choked, he dropped his cap. His joy was that of a child, unrestrained, unaffected, as genuine as gold. When they turned back to the veranda he eagerly drew up Bennett's chair for him, his eyes never leaving his face. It was the quivering, inarticulate affection of a dog for its master, faithful, submissive, unquestioning, happy for hours over a chance look, a kind word, a touch of the hand. To Adler's mind it would have been a privilege and an honour to have died for Bennett. Why, he was his chief, his king, his god, his master, who could do no wrong. Bennett could have slain him where he stood and Adler would still have trusted him.

Adler would not sit down until Bennett had twice ordered him to do so, and then he deposited himself in a nearby chair, in as uncomfortable a position as he could devise, allowing only the smallest fraction of his body to be supported as a mark of deference. He remained uncovered, and from time to time nervously saluted. But suddenly he remembered the object of his visit.

"Oh, but I forgot—seeing you like this, unexpected, sir, clean drove Mr. Ferriss out of my mind. How is he getting on? I saw in the papers he was main sick."

"He's dead," said Bennett quietly.

Adler was for the moment stricken speechless. His jaw dropped; he stared, and caught his breath.

"Mr. Ferriss dead!" he exclaimed at length. "I —I can't believe it." He crossed himself rapidly. Bennett made no reply, and for upward of five minutes the two men sat motionless in the chairs, looking off into the night. After a while Adler broke silence and asked a few questions as to Ferriss's sickness and the nature and time of his death —questions which Bennett answered as best he might. But it was evident that Bennett, alive and

present there in the flesh, was more to Adler than
Ferriss dead.

" But *you're* all right, sir, ain't you? " he asked
at length. " There ain't anything the matter with
you? "

" No," said Bennett, looking at him steadily ; then
suddenly he added :

" Adler, I was to blame for Mr. Ferriss's death.
If it hadn't been for me he would probably have
been alive to-night. It was my fault. I did what
I thought was right, when I knew all the time, just
as I know now, that I was wrong. So, when any
one asks you about Mr. Ferriss's death you are to
tell him just what you know about it—understand?
Through a mistake I was responsible for his death.
I shall not tell you more than that, but that much
you ought to know."

Adler looked at Bennett curiously and with infinite amazement. The order of his universe was
breaking up about his ears. Bennett, the inscruta-
ble, who performed his wonders in a mystery, im-
penetrable to common eyes, who moved with his
head in the clouds, behold ! he was rendering account
to him, Adler, the meanest of his subjects—the king
was condescending to the vassal, was admitting him
to his confidence. And what was this thing he was
saying, that he was responsible for Ferriss's death?
Adler did not understand ; his wits could not adjust
themselves to such information. Ferriss was dead,
but how was Bennett to blame? The king could
do no wrong. Adler did not understand. No
doubt Bennett was referring to something that had
happened during the retreat over the ice—some-

thing that had to be done, and that in the end, and after all this lapse of time, had brought about Mr. Ferriss's death. In any case Bennett had done what was right. For that matter he had been responsible for McPherson's death; but what else had there been to do?

Bennett had spoken as he did after a moment's rapid thinking. To Adler's questions as to the manner of the chief engineer's death Bennett had at first given evasive replies. But a sudden sense of shame at being compelled to dissemble before a subordinate had lashed him across the face. True, he had made a mistake—a fearful, unspeakable mistake—but at least let him be man enough to face and to accept its consequences. It might not be necessary or even expedient to make acknowledgment of his folly in all quarters, but at that moment it seemed to him that his men—at least one of them—who had been under the command of himself and his friend, had a right to be told the truth. It had been only one degree less distasteful to undeceive Adler than it had been to deceive him in the first place. Bennett was not the general to explain his actions to his men. But he had not hesitated a moment.

However, Adler was full of another subject, and soon broke out with:

"You know, sir, there's another expedition forming; I suppose you have heard—an English one. They call it the Duane-Parsons expedition. They are going to try the old route by Smith Sound. They are going to winter at Tasiusak, and try to get through the sound as soon as the ice breaks up in the spring. But Duane's ideas are all wrong. He'll make no very high northing, not above eighty-five. I'll bet a hat. When we go up again, sir, will you—will you let me—will you take me along? Did I give satisfaction this last——"

"I'm never going up again, Adler," answered Bennett.

"Sho!" said Adler a little blankly. "I thought sure—I never thought that you—why, there ain't no one else but you *can* do it, captain."

"Oh, yes, there is," said Bennett listlessly. "Duane can—if he has luck. I know him. He's a good man. No, I'm out of it, Adler; I had my chance. It is somebody else's turn now. Do you want to go with Duane? I can give you letters to him. He'd be glad to have you, I know."

Adler started from his place.

"Why, do you think—" he exclaimed vehemently—"do you think I'd go with anybody else but you, sir? Oh, you will be going some of these days, I'm sure of it. We—we'll have another try at it, sir, before we die. We ain't beaten yet."

"Yes, we are, Adler," returned Bennett, smiling calmly; "we'll stay at home now and write our book. But we'll let some one else reach the Pole. That's not for us—never will be, Adler."

At the end of their talk some half-hour later Adler stood up, remarking:

"Guess I'd better be standing by if I'm to get the last train back to the City to-night. They told me at the station that she'd clear about midnight." Suddenly he began to show signs of uneasiness, turning his cap about between his fingers, changing his weight from foot to foot. Then at length:

"You wouldn't be wanting a man about the place, would you, sir?" And before Bennett could reply he continued eagerly, "I've been a bit of most trades in my time, and I know how to take care of a garden like as you have here; I'm a main good hand with plants and flower things, and I could help around generally." Then, earnestly, "Let me stay, sir—it won't cost—I wouldn't think of taking a cent from you, captain. Just let me act as your orderly for a spell, sir. I'd sure give satisfaction; will you, sir—will you?"

"Nonsense, Adler," returned Bennett; "stay, if you like. I presume I can find use for you. But you must be paid, of course."

"Not a soomarkee," protested the other almost indignantly.

The next day Adler brought his chest down from the City and took up his quarters with Bennett at Medford. Though Dr. Pitts had long since ceased to keep horses, the stable still adjoined the house, and Adler swung his hammock in the coachman's old room. Bennett could not induce him to room in the house itself. Adler prided himself that he knew his place. After their first evening's conversation he never spoke to Bennett until spoken to first, and the resumed relationship of commander and subordinate was inexpressibly dear to him. It was something to see Adler waiting on the table in the "glass-room" in his blue jersey, standing at attention at the door, happy in the mere sight of Bennett at his meals. In the mornings, as soon as breakfast was ready, it was Adler's privilege to announce the fact to Bennett, whom he usually found already at work upon his writing. Returning thence to the dining-room, Adler waited for his lord to appear. As soon as he heard Bennett's step in the hall a little tremor of excitement possessed him. He ran to Bennett's chair, drawing it back for him, and as soon as Bennett had seated himself circled about him with all the pride and solicitude of a motherly hen. He opened his napkin for him, delivered him his paper, and pushed his cup of coffee a half-inch nearer his hand. Throughout the duration of the meal he hardly took his eyes from Bennett's face, watching his every movement with a glow of pride, his hands gently stroking one another in an excess of satisfaction and silent enjoyment.

The days passed; soon a fortnight was gone by. Drearily, mechanically, Bennett had begun work upon his book, the narrative of the expedition. It was repugnant to him. Long since he had lost all interest in polar exploration. As he had said to Adler, he was out of it, finally and irrevocably. His bolt was shot; his rôle upon the stage of the world was ended. He only desired now to be forgotten as quickly as possible, to lapse into mediocrity as easily and quietly as he could. Fame was nothing to him now. The thundering applause of an entire world that had once been his was mere noise, empty and meaningless. He did not care to reawaken it. The appearance of his book he knew was expected and waited for in every civilised nation of the globe. It would be printed in languages whereof he was ignorant, but it was all one with him now.

A Man's Woman

The task of writing was hateful to him beyond expression, but with such determination as he could yet summon to his aid Bennett stuck to it, eight, ten, and sometimes fourteen hours each day. In a way his narrative was an atonement. Ferriss was its hero. Almost instinctively Bennett kept the figure of himself, his own achievements, his own plans and ideas, in the background. On more than one page he deliberately ascribed to Ferriss triumphs which no one but himself had attained. It was Ferriss who was the leader, the victor to whom all laurels were due. It was Ferriss whose example had stimulated the expedition to its best efforts in the darkest hours; it was, practically, Ferriss who had saved the party after the destruction of the ship; whose determination, unbroken courage, endurance, and intelligence had pervaded all minds and hearts during the retreat to Kolyuchin Bay.

"Though nominally in command," wrote Bennett, "I continually gave place to him. Without his leadership we should all, unquestionably, have perished before even reaching land. His resolution to conquer, at whatever cost, was an inspiration to us all. Where he showed the way we had to follow; his courage was never daunted, his hope was never dimmed, his foresight, his intelligence, his ingenuity in meeting and dealing with apparently unsolvable problems were nothing short of marvellous. His was the genius of leadership. He was the explorer, born to his work."

One day, just after luncheon, as Bennett, according to his custom, was walking in the garden by the house, smoking a cigar before returning to his work, he was surprised to find himself bleeding at the nose. It was but a trifling matter, and passed off in a few moments, but the fact of its occurrence directed his attention to the state of his health, and he told himself that for the last few days he had not been at all his accustomed self. There had been dull pains in his back and legs; more than once his head had pained him, and of late the continuance of his work had been growing steadily more obnoxious to him, the very physical effort of driving the pen from line to line was a burden.

"Hum!" he said to himself later on in the day, when the bleeding at the nose returned upon him, "I think we need a little quinine."

But the next day he found he could not eat, and all the afternoon, though he held doggedly to his work, he was troubled with nausea. At times a great weakness, a relaxing of all the muscles, came over him. In the evening he sent a note to Dr. Pitts's address in the City, asking him to come down to Medford the next day.

.   .   .   .

On the Monday morning of the following week, some two hours after breakfast, Lloyd met Miss Douglass on the stairs, dressed for the street and carrying her nurse's bag.

"Are you going out?" she asked of the fever nurse in some astonishment. "Where are you going?" for Lloyd had returned to duty, and it was her name that now stood at the top of the list; "I thought it was my turn to go out," she added.

Miss Douglass was evidently much confused.

Her meeting with Lloyd had apparently been unexpected. She halted upon the stairs in great embarrassment, stammering:

"No—no, I'm on call. I—I was called out of my turn—specially called—that was it."

"Were you?" demanded Lloyd sharply, for the other nurse was disturbed to an extraordinary degree.

"Well, then; no, I wasn't, but the superintendent —Miss Bergyn—she thought—she advised—you had better see her."

"I will see her," declared Lloyd, "but don't you go till I find out why I was skipped."

Lloyd hurried at once to Miss Bergyn's room, indignant at this slight. Surely, after what had happened, she was entitled to more consideration than this. Of all the staff in the house she should have been the one to be preferred.

Miss Bergyn rose at Lloyd's sudden entrance into her room, and to her question responded:

"It was only because I wanted to spare you further trouble and—and embarrassment, Lloyd, that I told Miss Douglass to take your place. This call is from Medford. Dr. Pitts was here himself this morning, and he thought as I did."

"Thought what? I don't understand."

"It seemed to me," answered the superintendent nurse, "that this one case of all others would be the hardest, the most disagreeable for you to take. It seems that Mr. Bennett has leased Dr. Pitts's house from him. He is there now. At the time when Mr. Ferriss was beginning to be ill Mr. Bennett was with him a great deal and undertook to nurse

him till Dr. Pitts interfered and put a professional
nurse on the case. Since then, too, the doctor has
found out that Mr. Bennett has exposed himself im-
prudently. At any rate, in some way he has contracted the same disease and is rather seriously
ill with it. Dr. Pitts wants us to send him a nurse
at once. It just happened that it was your turn,
and I thought I had better skip your name and send
Louise Douglass."

Lloyd sank into a chair, her hands falling limply
in her lap. A frown of perplexity gathered on her
forehead. But suddenly she exclaimed:

" I know—that's all as it may be; but all the staff
know that it is my turn to go; everybody in the
house knows who is on call. How will it be—
what will be thought when it is known that I haven't
gone—and after—after my failing once—after this
—this other affair? No, I must go. I, of all people,
must go—and just because it is a typhoid case, like
the other."

" But, Lloyd, how _can_ you? "

True, how could she? Her patient would be the
same man who had humiliated her and broken her,
had so cruelly misunderstood and wronged her, for
whom all her love was dead. How could she face
him again? Yet how refuse to take the case? How
explain a second failure to her companions? Lloyd
made a little movement of distress, clasping her
hands together. How the complications followed
fast upon each other! No sooner was one difficult
situation met and disposed of than another presented itself. Bennett was nothing to her now, yet,
for all that, she recoiled instinctively from meeting

him again. Not only must she meet him, but she must be with him day after day, hour after hour, at his very side, in all the intimacy that the sick-room involved. On the other hand, how could she decline this case? The staff might condone one apparent and inexplicable defection; another would certainly not be overlooked. But was not this new situation a happy and unlooked-for opportunity to vindicate her impaired prestige in the eyes of her companions? Lloyd made up her mind upon the instant. She rose.

" I shall take the case," she said.

She was not a little surprised at herself. Hardly an instant had she hesitated. On that other occasion when she had believed it right to make confession to her associates it had been hard—at times almost impossible—for her to do her duty as she saw and understood it. This new complication was scarcely less difficult, but once having attained the fine, moral rigour that had carried her through her former ordeal, it became easy now to do right under all or any circumstances, however adverse. If she had failed then, she certainly would have failed now. That she had succeeded then made it all the easier to succeed now. Dimly Lloyd commenced to understand that the mastery of self, the steady, firm control of natural, intuitive impulses, selfish because natural, was a progression. Each victory not only gained the immediate end in view, but braced the mind and increased the force of will for the next shock, the next struggle. She had imagined and had told herself that Bennett had broken her strength for good. But was it really so? Had not defeat in that case been only temporary? Was she not slowly getting back her strength by an unflinching adherence to the simple, fundamental principles of right, and duty, and truth? Was not the struggle with one's self the greatest fight of all, greater, far greater, than had been the conflict between Bennett's will and her own?

Within the hour she found herself once again on her way to Medford. How much had happened, through what changes had she passed since the occasion of her first journey; and Bennett, how he, too, changed; how different he had come to stand in her estimation! Once the thought that he was in danger had been a constant terror to her, and haunted her days and lurked at her side through many a waking night. Was it possible that now his life or death was no more to her than that of any of her former patients? She could not say; she avoided answering the question. Certainly her heart beat no faster at this moment to know that he was in the grip of a perilous disease. She told herself that her Bennett was dead already; that she was coming back to Medford not to care for and watch over the individual, but to combat the disease.

When she arrived at the doctor's house in Medford, a strange-looking man opened the door for her, and asked immediately if she was the nurse.

"Yes," said Lloyd, "I am. Is Dr. Pitts here?"

"Upstairs in his room," answered the other in a whisper, closing the front door with infinite softness. "He won't let me go in, the doctor won't; I—I ain't seen him in four days. Ask the doctor if I

can't just have a blink at him—just a little blink
through the crack of the door. Just think, Miss, I
ain't seen him in four days! Just think of that!
And look here, they ain't giving him enough to eat
—nothing but milk and chicken soup with rice in it.
He never did like rice; that's no kind of rations for
a sick man. I fixed him up a bit of duff yesterday,
what he used to like so much aboard ship, and Pitts
wouldn't let him have it. He regularly laughed in
my face."

Lloyd sent word to the doctor by the housekeeper
that she had arrived, and on going up found Pitts
waiting for her at the door of the sick-room, not
that which had been occupied by Ferriss, but
another—the guest-chamber of the house, situated
toward the rear of the building.

"Why, I expected Miss Douglass!" exclaimed
the doctor in a low voice as soon as his eye fell upon
Lloyd. "Any one of them but you!"

"I had to come," Lloyd answered quietly, flushing hotly for all that. "It was my turn, and it was
not right for me to stay away."

The doctor hesitated an instant, and then dismissed the subject, putting his chin in the air as if
to say that, after all, it was not his affair.

"Well," he said, "it's queer to see how things
will tangle themselves sometimes. I don't know
whether he took this thing from Ferriss or not.
Both of them were exposed to the same conditions
when their expedition went to pieces and they were
taken off by the whaling ships—bad water, weakened constitution, not much power of resistance; in
prime condition for the bacillus, and the same cause

might have produced the same effect; at any rate, he's in a bad way."

" Is he—very bad? " asked Lloyd.

" Well, he's not the hang-on sort that Mr. Ferriss was; nothing undecided about Captain Ward Bennett; when he's sick, he's sick; rushes right at it like a blind bull. He's as bad now as Mr. Ferriss was in his third week."

" Do you think he will recognise me? "

The doctor shook his head. " No; delirious most of the time—of course—regulation thing. If we don't keep the fever down he'll go out sure. That's the danger in his case. Look at him yourself; here he is. The devil! The animal is sitting up again."

As Lloyd entered the room she saw Bennett sitting bolt upright in his bed, staring straight before him, his small eyes, with their deforming cast, open to their fullest extent, the fingers of his shrunken, bony hands dancing nervously on the coverlet. A week's growth of stubble blackened the lower part of his face. Without a moment's pause he mumbled and muttered with astonishing rapidity, but for the most part the words were undistinguishable. It was, indeed, not the same Bennett, Lloyd had last seen. The great body was collapsed upon itself; the skin of the face was like dry, brown parchment, and behind it the big, massive bones stood out in great knobs and ridges. It needed but a glance to know that here was a man dangerously near to his death. While Lloyd was removing her hat and preparing herself for her work the doctor got Bennett upon his back again and replenished the ice-pack about his head.

"Not much strength left in our friend now," he murmured.

"How long has he been like this?" asked Lloyd as she arranged the contents of her nurse's bag on a table near the window.

"Pretty close to eight hours now. He was conscious yesterday morning, however, for a little while, and wanted to know what his chances were."

They were neither good nor many; the strength once so formidable was ebbing away like a refluent tide, and that with ominous swiftness. Stimulate the life as the doctor would, strive against the enemy's advance as Lloyd might, Bennett continued to sink.

"The devil of it is," muttered the doctor, "that he don't seem to care. He had as soon give up as not. It's hard to save a patient that don't want to save himself. If he'd fight for his life as he did in the arctic, we could pull him through yet. Otherwise——" he shrugged his shoulders almost helplessly.

The next night toward nine o'clock Lloyd took the doctor's place at their patient's bedside, and Pitts, without taking off his clothes, stretched himself out upon the sofa in one of the rooms on the lower floor of the house, with the understanding that the nurse was to call him in case of any change.

But as the doctor was groping his way down the darkened stairway he stumbled against Adler and Kamiska. Adler was sitting on one of the steps, and the dog was on her haunches close at his side; the two were huddled together there in the dark, broad awake, shoulder to shoulder, waiting, watching, and listening for the faint sounds that came at long intervals from the direction of the room where Bennett lay.

As the physician passed him Adler stood up and saluted:

"Is he doing any better now, sir?" he whispered.

"Nothing new," returned the other brusquely, "He may get well in three weeks' time or he may die before midnight; so there you are. You know as much about it as I do. Damn that dog!"

He trod upon Kamiska, who forbore heroically to yelp, and went on his way. Adler resumed his place on the stairs, sitting down gingerly, so that the boards should not creak under his weight. He took Kamiska's head between his hands and rocked himself gently to and fro.

"What are we going to do, little dog?" he whispered. "What are we going to do if—if our captain should—if he shouldn't——" he had no words to finish. Kamiska took her place again by his side, and the two resumed their vigil.

Meanwhile, not fifty feet away, a low voice, monotonous and rapid, was keeping up a continuous, murmuring flow of words.

"That's well your number two sledge. All hands on the McClintock now. You've got to do it, men. Forward, get forward, get forward; get on to the south, always to the south—south, south, south! . . . There, there's the ice again. That's the biggest ridge yet. At it now! Smash through; I'll break you yet; believe me, I will! There, we broke it! I knew you could, men. I'll pull you through. Now, then, h'up your other sledge. For-

ward! There will be double rations to-night all
round—no—half-rations, quarter-rations . . .
No, three-fifths of an ounce of dog-meat and a
spoonful of alcohol—that's all; that's all, men.
Pretty cold night, this—minus thirty-eight.   Only
a quarter of a mile covered to-day. Everybody
suffering in their feet, and so weak—and starving—
and freezing."   All at once the voice became a wail.
" My God! is it never going to end? . . . Sh—h,
steady, what was that? Who whimpered? Was
that Ward Bennett?   No whimpering, whatever
comes. Stick it out like men, anyway. Fight it
out till we drop, but no whimpering. . . . Who
said there were steam whalers off the floe? That's
a lie! Forward, forward, get forward to the south
—no, not the south; to the *north*, to the north!
We'll reach it, we'll succeed; we're most there, men;
come on, come on! I tell you this time we'll reach
it; one more effort, men! We're most there!
What's the latitude? Eighty-five-twenty—eighty-
six."   The voice began to grow louder: " Come
on, men; we're most there! Eighty-seven—eighty-
eight—eighty-nine-twenty-five!" He rose to a sitting position.   " Eighty-nine-thirty—eighty-nine-
forty-five." Suddenly the voice rose to a shout.
"Ninety degrees! *By God, it's the Pole!* "
The voice died away to indistinct mutterings.
Lloyd was at the bedside by now, and quietly
pressed Bennett down upon his back.   But as she
did so a thrill of infinite pity and compassion quivered through her. She had forced him down so
easily. He was so pitifully weak. Woman though
she was, she could, with one small hand upon his

breast, control this man who at one time had been
of such colossal strength—such vast physical force.

Suddenly Bennett began again. "Where's Ferriss? Where's Richard Ferriss? Where's the chief
engineer of the Freja Arctic Exploring Expedition?"

He fell silent again, and but for the twitching,
dancing hands, lay quiet. Then he cried:

"Attention to the roll-call!"

Rapidly and in a low voice he began calling off
the muster of the Freja's men and officers, giving
the answers himself.

"Adler—here; Blair—here; Dahl—here; Fishbaugh—here; Hawes—here; McPherson—here;
Muck Tu—here; Woodward—here; Captain Ward
Bennett—here; Dr. Sheridan Dennison—here;
Chief Engineer Richard Ferriss——" no answer.
Bennett waited for a moment, then repeated the
name, "Chief Engineer Richard Ferriss——"
Again he was silent; but after a few seconds he
called aloud in agony of anxiety, "Chief Engineer
Richard Ferriss, answer to the roll-call!"

Then once more he began; his disordered wits
calling to mind a different order of things:

"Adler—here; Blair—died from exhaustion at
Point Kane; Dahl—here; Fishbaugh—starved to
death on the march to Kolyuchin Bay; Hawes—
died of arctic fever at Cape Kammeni; McPherson
—unable to keep up, and abandoned at ninth camp;
Muck Tu—here; Woodward—died from starvation
at twelfth camp; Dr. Sheridan Dennison—frozen to
death at Kolyuchin Bay; Chief Engineer Richard
Ferriss—died by the act of his best friend, Captain

Ward Bennett!" Again and again Bennett repeated this phrase, calling: "Richard Ferriss! Richard Ferriss!" and immediately adding in a broken voice: "Died by the act of his best friend, Captain Ward Bennett." Or at times it was only the absence of Ferriss that seemed to torture him. He would call the roll, answering "here" to each name until he reached Ferriss; then he would not respond, but instead would cry aloud over and over again, in accents of the bitterest grief, "Richard Ferriss, answer to the roll-call; Richard Ferriss, answer to the roll-call——" Then suddenly, with a feeble, quavering cry, "For God's sake, Dick, answer to the roll-call!"

The hours passed. Ten o'clock struck, then eleven. At midnight Lloyd took the temperature (which had decreased considerably) and the pulse, and refilled the ice-pack about the head. Bennett was still muttering in the throes of delirium, still calling for Ferriss, imploring him to answer to the roll-call; or repeating the words: "Dick Ferriss, chief engineer—died at the hands of his best friend, Ward Bennett," in tones so pitiful, so heart-broken that more than once Lloyd felt the tears running down her cheeks.

"Richard Ferriss, Richard Ferriss, answer to the roll-call; Dick, old man, won't you answer, won't you answer, old chap, when I call you? Won't you come back and say 'It's all right?' Ferriss, Ferriss, answer to my roll-call. . . . Died at the hands of his best friend. . . . At Kolyuchin Bay. . . . Killed, and I did it. . . . Forward, men; you've *got* to do it; snowing to-day and all the ice in motion. . . . H'up y'r other sledge. Come on with y'r number four; more pressure-ridges; I'll break you yet! Come on with y'r number four! . . . Lloyd Searight, what are you doing in this room?"

On the instant the voice had changed from confused mutterings to distinct, clear-cut words. The transition was so sudden that Lloyd, at the moment busy at her nurse's bag, her back to the bed, wheeled sharply about to find Bennett sitting bolt upright, looking straight at her with intelligent, wide-open eyes. Lloyd's heart for an instant stood still, almost in terror. This sudden leap back from the darkness of delirium into the daylight of consciousness was almost like a rising from the dead, ghost-like, appalling. She caught her breath, trembling in spite of her best efforts, and for an instant leaned a hand upon the table behind her.

But on Bennett's face, ghastly, ravaged by disease, with its vast, protruding jaw, its narrow, contracted forehead and unkempt growth of beard, the dawning of intelligence and surprise swiftly gave place to an expression of terrible anxiety and apprehension.

" What are you doing here, Lloyd?" he cried.

" Hush!" she answered quickly as she came forward; "above all things you must not sit up; lie down again and don't talk. You are very sick."

" I know, I know," he answered feebly. " I know what it is. But you must leave here. It's a terrible risk every moment you stay in this room. I want you to go. You understand—at once! Call the doctor. Don't come near the bed," he went on excitedly, struggling to keep himself from sinking back upon the pillows. His breath was coming quick; his eyes were flashing. All the poor, shattered senses were aroused and quivering with excitement and dread.

"It will kill you to stay here," he continued, almost breathless. "Out of this room!" he commanded. "Out of this house! It is mine now; I'm the master here—do you understand? Don't!" he exclaimed as Lloyd put her hands upon his shoulders to force him to lie down again.

"Don't, don't touch me! Stand away from me!"

He tried to draw back from her in the bed. Then suddenly he made a great effort to rise, resisting her efforts.

"I shall put you out, then," he declared, struggling against Lloyd's clasp upon his shoulders, catching at her wrists. His excitement was so intense, his fervour so great that it could almost be said he touched the edge of his delirium again.

"Do you hear, do you hear? Out of this room!"

"No," said Lloyd calmly; "you must be quiet; you must try to go to sleep. This time you cannot make me leave."

He caught her by one arm, and, bracing himself with the other against the headboard of the bed, thrust her back from him with all his might.

"Keep away from me, I tell you; keep back! You shall do as I say! I have always carried my point, and I shall not fail now. Believe me, I shall not. You—you——" he panted as he struggled with her, ashamed of his weakness, humiliated beyond words that she should know it. "I—you shall——

you will compel me to use force.   Don't let it come
to that."

Calmly Lloyd took both his wrists in the strong,
quiet clasp of one palm, and while she supported his
shoulders with her other arm, laid him down
among the pillows again as though he had been a
child.

" I'm—I'm a bit weak and trembly just now," he
admitted, panting with his exertion; " but, Lloyd,
listen.   I know how you must dislike me now, but
will you please go—go, go at once!"

" No."

What a strange spinning of the wheel of fate was
here!   In so short a time had their mutual positions
been reversed.   Now it was she who was strong and
he who was weak.   It was she who conquered and
he who was subdued.   It was she who triumphed
and he who was humiliated.   It was he who im-
plored and she who denied.   It was her will and no
longer his that must issue victorious from the
struggle.

And how complete now was Bennett's defeat!
The very contingency he had fought so desperately
to avert and for which he had sacrificed Ferriss—
Lloyd's care of so perilous a disease—behold! the
mysterious turn of the wheel had brought it about,
and now he was powerless to resist.

" Oh!" he cried, " have I not enough upon my
mind already—Ferriss and his death?   Are you going to make me imperil your life too, and after I
have tried so hard?   You must not stay here."

" I shall stay," she answered.

" I order you to go.   This is my house.   Send

the doctor here. Where's Adler?" Suddenly he
fainted.

An hour or two later, in the gray of the morning,
at a time when Bennett was sleeping quietly under
the influence of opiates, Lloyd found herself sitting
at the window in front of the small table there, her
head resting on her hand, thoughtful, absorbed, and
watching with but half-seeing eyes the dawn growing pink over the tops of the apple-trees in the
orchard near by.

The window was open just wide enough for the
proper ventilation of the room. For a long time
she sat thus without moving, only from time to time
smoothing back the heavy, bronze-red hair from her
temples and ears. By degrees the thinking faculties
of her brain, as it were, a myriad of delicate inter-
lacing wheels, slowly decreased in the rapidity and
intensity of their functions. She began to feel instead of to think. As the activity of her mind lapsed
to a certain pleasant numbness, a vague, formless,
nameless emotion seemed to be welling to the surface. It was no longer a question of the brain.
What then? Was it the heart? She gave no name
to this new emotion.; it was too confused as yet,
too undefinable. A certain great sweetness seemed
to be coming upon her, but she could not say
whether she was infinitely sad or supremely happy;
a smile was on her lips, and yet the tears began to
brim in her dull-blue eyes.

She felt as if some long, fierce struggle, or series
of struggles, were at last accomplished; as if for a
long period of time she had been involved in the
maze and tortuous passages of some gloomy cavern,

but at length, thence issuing, had again beheld the stars. A great tenderness, a certain tremulous joy in all things that were true and good and right, grew big and strong within her; the delight in living returned to her. The dawn was brightening and flushing over all the world, and colour, light, and warmth were coming back into her life. The night had been still and mild, but now the first breath of the morning breeze stirred in the trees, in the grass, in the flowers, and the thick, dew-drenched bushes along the roadside, and a delicious aroma of fields and woods and gardens came to her. The sweetness of life and the sweetness of those things better than life and more enduring, the things that do not fail, nor cease, nor vanish away, suddenly entered into that room and descended upon her almost in the sense of a benediction, a visitation, something mystic and miraculous. It was a moment to hope all things, to believe all things, to endure all things.

She caught her breath, listening—for what she did not know. Once again, just as it had been in that other dawn, in that other room where the Enemy had been conquered, the sense of some great happiness was in the air, was coming to her swiftly. But now the greater Enemy had been outfought, the morning of a greater day was breaking and spreading, and the greatest happiness in the world was preparing for her. How it had happened she did not know. Now was not the moment to think, to reason, to reflect. It seemed as though the rushing of wings was all about her, as though a light brighter than the day was just about to break upon her sight, as though a music divinely beautiful was just about to burst upon her ear. But the light was not for her eye; the music was not for her ear. The radiance and the harmony came from herself, from within her. The intellect was numb. Only the heart was alive on this wonderful midsummer's morning, and it was in her heart that the radiance shone and the harmony vibrated. Back in his place once more, high on his throne, the love that she believed had forever departed from her sat exalted and triumphant, singing to the cadence of that unheard music, shining and magnificent in the glory of that new-dawned light.

Would Bennett live? Suddenly that question leaped up in her mind and stood in the eye of her imagination, terrible, menacing—a hideous, grim spectre, before which Lloyd quailed with failing heart and breath. The light, the almost divine radiance that had burst upon her, nevertheless threw a dreadful shadow before it. Beneath the music she heard the growl of the thunder. Her new-found happiness was not without its accompanying dismay. Love had not returned to her heart alone. With it had returned the old Enemy she had once believed had left her forever. Now it had come back. As before, it lurked and leered at her from dark corners. It crept to her side, to her back, ready to leap, ready to strike, to clutch at her throat with cold fingers and bear her to the earth, rending her heart with a grief she told herself she could not endure and live. She loved him now with all her mind and might; how could it ever have been otherwise? He belonged to her—and she? Why, she only lived with his life; she seemed so bound to him as to be part of his very self. Literally, she could not understand how it would be possible for her to live if he should die. It seemed to her that with his death some mysterious element of her life, something vital and fundamental, for which there was no name, would disintegrate upon the instant and leave her without the strength necessary for further existence. But this would, however, be a relief. The prospect of the years after his death, the fearful loneliness of life without him, was a horror before which she veritably believed her reason itself must collapse.

" Lloyd."

Bennett was awake again and watching her with feverish anxiety from where he lay among the pillows. " Lloyd," he repeated, the voice once so deep and powerful quavering pitifully. " I was wrong. I don't want you to go. Don't leave me."

In an instant Lloyd was at his side, kneeling by the bed. She caught one of the great, gnarled hands, seamed and corded and burning with the fever. " Never, never, dearest; never so long as I shall live."

IX.

When Adler heard Bennett's uncertain steps upon
the stairs and the sound of Lloyd's voice speaking
to him and urging that there was no hurry, and that
he was to take but one step at a time, he wheeled
swiftly about from the windows of the glass-room,
where he had been watching the October breeze
stirring the crimson and yellow leaves in the orchard, and drew back his master's chair from the
breakfast table and stood behind it expectantly, his
eyes watching the door.

Lloyd held back the door, and Bennett came in,
leaning heavily on Dr. Pitts's shoulder.   Adler
stiffened upon the instant as if in answer to some
unheard bugle-call, and when Bennett had taken
his seat, pushed his chair gently to the table and
unfolded his napkin with a flourish as though giving
a banner to the wind.   Pitts almost immediately left
the room, but Lloyd remained supervising Bennett's
breakfast, pouring his milk, buttering his toast, and
opening his eggs.

"Coffee?" suddenly inquired Bennett.   Lloyd
shook her head.

"Not for another week."

Bennett looked with grim disfavour upon the
glass of milk that Lloyd had placed at his elbow.

"Such slop!" he growled.   "Why not a little
sugar and warm water, and be done with it?   Lloyd,

I can't drink this stuff any more. Why, it's warm yet!" he exclaimed aggrievedly and with deep disgust, abruptly setting down the glass.

"Why, of course it is," she answered; "we brought the cow here especially for you, and the boy has just done milking her—and it's not slop."

"Slop! slop!" declared Bennett. He picked up the glass again and looked at her over the rim.

"I'll drink this stuff this one more time to please you," he said. "But I promise you this will be the last time. You needn't ask me again. I have drunk enough milk the past three weeks to support a foundling hospital for a year."

Invariably, since the period of his convalescence began, Bennett made this scene over his hourly glass of milk, and invariably it ended by his gulping it down at nearly a single swallow.

Adler brought in the mail and the morning paper. Three letters had come for Lloyd, and for Bennett a small volume on " Recent Arctic Research and Exploration," sent by his publisher with a note to the effect that, as the latest authority on the subject, Bennett was sure to find it of great interest. In an appendix, inserted after the body of the book had been made up, the Freja expedition and his own work were briefly described. Lloyd put her letters aside, and, unfolding the paper, said, "I'll read it while you eat your breakfast. Have you everything you want? Did you drink your milk—all of it?" But out of the corner of her eye she noted that Adler was chuckling behind the tray that he held to his face, and with growing suspicion she leaned forward

and peered about among the breakfast things.
Bennett had hidden his glass behind the toast-rack.

"And it's only two-thirds empty," she declared.
"Ward, why will you be such a boy?"

"Oh, well," he grumbled, and without more ado
drank off the balance.

"Now I'll read to you if you have everything
you want. Adler, I think you can open one of those
windows; it's so warm out of doors."

While he ate his breakfast of toast, milk, and eggs
Lloyd skimmed through the paper, reading aloud
everything she thought would be of interest to him.
Then, after a moment, her eye was caught and held
by a half-colmun article expanded from an Associated Press despatch.

"Oh!" she cried, "listen to this!" and continued: "'Word has been received at this place of
the safe arrival of the arctic steamship Curlew
at Tasiusak, on the Greenland coast, bearing eighteen members of the Duane-Parsons expedition.
Captain Duane reports all well and an uneventful
voyage. It is his intention to pass the winter at
Tasiusak, collecting dogs and also Esquimau
sledges, which he believes superior to European
manufacture for work in rubble-ice, and to push
on with the Curlew in the spring as soon as
Smith Sound shall be navigable. This may be later
than Captain Duane supposes, as the whalers who
have been working in the sound during the past
months bring back news of an unusually early winter and extraordinary quantities of pack-ice both
in the sound itself and in Kane Basin. This means
a proportionately late open season next year, and

the Curlew's departure from Tasiusak may be considerably later than anticipated. It is considered by the best arctic experts an unfortunate circumstance that Captain Duane elected to winter south of Cape Sabine, as the condition of the ice in Smith Sound can never be relied upon nor foretold. Should the entrance to the sound still be encumbered with ice as late as July, which is by no means impossible, Captain Duane will be obliged to spend another winter at Tasiusak or Upernvick, consuming alike his store of provisions and the patience of his men.' "

There was a silence when Lloyd finished reading. Bennett chipped at the end of his second egg.

" Well? " she said at length.

" Well," returned Bennett, " what's all that to me? "

" It's your work," she answered almost vehemently.

" No, indeed. It's Duane's work."

" What do you mean? "

" Let him try now."

" And you? " exclaimed Lloyd, looking intently at him.

" My dear girl, I had my chance and failed. Now—" he raised a shoulder indifferently—" now, I don't care much about it. I've lost interest."

" I don't believe you," she cried energetically; " you of all men." Behind Bennett's chair she had a momentary glimpse of Adler, who had tucked his tray under his arm and was silently applauding in elaborate pantomime. She saw his lips form the words " That's it; that's right. Go right ahead."

" Besides, I have my book to do, and, besides that, I'm an invalid—an invalid who drinks slop."

" And you intend to give it all up—your career?"

" Well—if I should, what then?" Suddenly he turned to her abruptly. " I should not think *you* would want me to go again. Do *you* urge me to go?"

Lloyd made a sudden little gasp, and her hand involuntarily closed upon his as it rested near her on the table.

" Oh, no!" she cried. " Oh, no, I don't! You are right. It's not your work now."

" Well, then," muttered Bennett as though the question was forever settled.

Lloyd turned to her mail, and one after another slit the envelopes, woman fashion, with a shell hairpin. But while she was glancing over the contents of her letters Bennett began to stir uneasily in his place. From time to time he stopped eating and shot a glance at Lloyd from under his frown, noting the crisp, white texture of her gown and waist, the white scarf with its high, tight bands about the neck, the tiny, golden buttons in her cuffs, the sombre, ruddy glow of her cheeks, her dull-blue eyes, and the piles and coils of her bronze-red hair. Then, abruptly, he said:

" Adler, you can go."

Adler saluted and withdrew.

" Whom are your letters from?" Bennett demanded by way of a beginning.

Lloyd replaced the hairpin in her hair, answering:

" From Dr. Street, from Louise Douglass, and from—Mr. Campbell."

"Hum! well, what do they say? Dr. Street and
—Louise Douglass?"

"Dr. Street asks me to take a very important
surgical case as soon as I get through here, 'one of
the most important and delicate, as well as one of
the most interesting, operations in his professional
experience.' Those are his words. Louise writes
four pages, but she says nothing; just chatters."

"And Campbell?" Bennett indicated with his
chin the third rather voluminous letter at Lloyd's
elbow. "He seems to have written rather more
than four pages. What does he say? Does he
'chatter' too?"

Lloyd smoothed back her hair from one temple.

"H'm—no. He says—something. But never
mind what he says. Ward, I must be going back
to the City. You don't need a nurse any more."

"What's that?" Bennett's frown gathered on
the instant, and with a sharp movement of the head
that was habitual to him he brought his one good
eye to bear upon her.

Lloyd repeated her statement, answering his re-
monstrance and expostulation with:

"You are almost perfectly well, and it would not
be at all—discreet for me to stay here an hour longer
than absolutely necessary. I shall go back to-
morrow or next day."

"But, I tell you, I am still very sick. I'm a poor,
miserable, shattered wreck."

He made a great show of coughing in hollow,
lamentable tones.

"Listen to that, and last night I had a high fever,
and this morning I had a queer sort of pain about

here—" he vaguely indicated the region of his chest. " I think I am about to have a relapse."

" Nonsense! You can't frighten me at all."

" Oh, well," he answered easily, " I shall go with you—that is all. I suppose you want to see me venture out in such raw, bleak weather as this—with my weak lungs."

" Your weak lungs? How long since?"

" Well, I—I've sometimes thought my lungs were not very strong."

" Why, dear me, you poor thing; I suppose the climate at Kolyuchin Bay *was* a trifle too bracing——"

" What does Campbell say?"

" ——and the diet too rich for your blood——"

" What does Campbell say?"

" ——and perhaps you did overexert——"

" Lloyd Searight, what does Mr. Campbell say in that——"

" He asks me to marry him."

" To mum—mar—marry him? Well, damn his impudence!"

" Mr. Campbell is an eminently respectable and worthy gentleman."

" Oh, well, I don't care. Go! Go, marry Mr. Campbell. Be happy. I forgive you both. Go, leave me to die alone."

" Sir, I will go. Forget that you ever knew an unhappy wom—female, whose only fault was that she loved you."

" Go! and sometimes think of me far away on the billow and drop a silent tear—I say, how are you going to answer Campbell's letter?"

A Man's Woman

"Just one word—'*Come.*'"

"Lloyd, be serious. This is no joke."

"Joke!" she repeated hollowly. "It is, indeed, a sorry joke. Ah! had I but loved with a girlish love, it would have been better for me."

Then suddenly she caught him about the neck with both her arms, and kissed him on the cheek and on the lips, a little quiver running through her to her finger-tips, her mood changing abruptly to a deep, sweet earnestness.

"Oh, Ward, Ward!" she cried, "all our unhappiness and all our sorrow and trials and anxiety and cruel suspense are over now, and now we really have each other and love each other, dear, and all the years to come are only going to bring happiness to us, and draw us closer and nearer to each other."

"But here's a point, Lloyd," said Bennett after a few moments and when they had returned to coherent speech; "how about your work? You talk about my career; what about yours? We are to be married, but I know just how you have loved your work. It will be a hard wrench for you if you give that up. I am not sure that I should ask it of you. This letter of Street's, now. I know just how eager you must be to take charge of such operations— such important cases as he mentions. It would be very selfish of me to ask you to give up your work. It's your life-work, your profession, your career."

Lloyd took up Dr. Street's letter, and, holding it delicately at arm's length, tore it in two and let the pieces flutter to the floor.

"That, for my life-work," said Lloyd Searight.

As she drew back from him an instant later Bennett all at once and very earnestly demanded:

" Lloyd, do you love me? "

" With all my heart, Ward. "

" And you will be my wife? "

" You know that I will. "

" Then "—Bennett picked up the little volume of " Arctic Research " which he had received that morning, and tossed it from him upon the floor—" that, for my career," he answered.

For a moment they were silent, looking gladly into each other's eyes. Then Bennett drew her to him again and held her close to him, and once more she put her arms around his neck and nestled her head down upon his shoulder with a little comfortable sigh of contentment and relief and quiet joy, for that the long, fierce trial was over; that there were no more fights to be fought, no more grim, hard situations to face, no more relentless duties to be done. She had endured and she had prevailed; now her reward was come. Now for the long, calm years of happiness.

Later in the day, about an hour after noon, Bennett took his daily nap, carefully wrapped in shawls and stretched out in a wicker steamer-chair in the glass-room. Lloyd, in the meantime, was busy in the garden at the side of the house, gathering flowers which she intended to put in a huge china bowl in Bennett's room. While she was thus occupied Adler, followed by Kamiska, came up. Adler pulled off his cap.

" I beg pardon, Miss," he began, turning his cap about between his fingers. " I don't want to seem

to intrude, and if I do I just guess you'd better tell
me so first off. But what did he say—or did he say
anything—the captain, I mean—this morning about
going up again? I heard you talking to him at
breakfast. That's it, that's the kind of talk he
needs. I can't talk that talk to him. I'm so main
scared of him. I wouldn't 'a' believed the captain
would ever say he'd give up, would ever say he was
beaten. But, Miss, I'm thinking as there's something wrong, main wrong with the captain these
days besides fever. He's getting soft—that's what
he is. If you'd only know the man that he was—
before—while we was up there in the Ice! That's
his work, that's what he's cut out for. There ain't
nobody can do it but him, and to see him quit, to see
him chuck up his chance to a third-rate ice-pilot
like Duane—a coastwise college professor that don't
know no more about Ice than—than you do—it
regularly makes me sick. Why, what will become
of the captain now if he quits? He'll just settle
down to an ordinary stay-at-home, write-in-a-book
professor, and write articles for the papers and magazines, and bye-and-bye, maybe, he'll get down to
lecturing! Just fancy, Miss, him, the captain, lecturing! And while he stays at home and writes,
and—oh, Lord!—lectures, somebody else, without a
fifth of his ability, will do the *work*. It'll just naturally break my heart, it will!" exclaimed Adler,
" if the captain chucks. I wouldn't be so main sorry
that he won't reach the Pole as that he quit trying—
as that a man like the captain—or like what I
thought he was—gave up and chucked when he
could win."

A Man's Woman

"But, Adler," returned Lloyd, "the captain—Mr. Bennett, it seems to me, has done his share. Think what he's been through. *You* can't have forgotten the march to Kolyuchin Bay?"

But Adler made an impatient gesture with the hand that held the cap. "The danger don't figure; what he'd have to go through with don't figure; the chances of life or death don't figure; nothing in the world don't figure. *It's his work;* God A'mighty cut him out for that, and he's got to do it. Ain't you got any influence with him, Miss? Won't you talk good talk to him? Don't let him chuck; don't let him get soft. Make him be a Man and not a professor."

When Adler had left her Lloyd sank into a little seat at the edge of the garden walk, and let the flowers drop into her lap, and leaned back in her place, wide-eyed and thoughtful, reviewing in her imagination the events of the past few months. What a change that summer had brought to both of them; how they had been shaped anew in the mould of circumstance!

Suddenly and without warning, they two, high-spirited, strong, determined, had clashed together, the man's force against the woman's strength; and the woman, inherently weaker, had been crushed and humbled. For a time it seemed to her that she had been broken beyond hope; so humbled that she could never rise again; as though a great crisis had developed in her life, and that, having failed once, she must fail again, and again, and again—as if her whole subsequent life must be one long failure. But a greater crisis had followed hard upon the heels of the first—the struggle with self, the greatest struggle of all. Against the abstract principle of evil the woman who had failed in the material conflict with a masculine, masterful will, had succeeded, had conquered self, had been true when it was easy to be false, had dared the judgment of her peers so only that she might not deceive.

Her momentary, perhaps fancied, hatred of Bennett, who had so cruelly misunderstood and humiliated her, had apparently, of its own accord, departed from her heart. Then had come the hour when the strange hazard of fortune had reversed their former positions, when she could be masterful while he was weak; when it was the man's turn to be broken, to be prevailed against. Her own discomfiture had been offset by his. She no longer need look to him as her conqueror, her master. And when she had seen him so weak, so pathetically unable to resist the lightest pressure of her hand; when it was given her not only to witness but to relieve his suffering, the great love for him that could not die had returned. With the mastery of self had come the forgetfulness of self; and her profession, her life-work, of which she had been so proud, had seemed to her of small concern. Now she was his, and his life was hers. She should—so she told herself—be henceforward happy in his happiness, and her only pride would be the pride in his achievements.

But now the unexpected had happened, and Bennett had given up his career. During the period of Bennett's convalescence Lloyd had often talked long and earnestly with him, and partly from what he had told her and partly from much that she inferred she had at last been able to trace out and follow the mental processes and changes through which Bennett had passed. He, too, had been proved by fire; he, too, had had his ordeal, his trial.

By nature, by training, and by virtue of the life he lived Bennett had been a man, harsh, somewhat brutal, inordinately selfish, and at all times magnificently arrogant. He had neither patience nor toleration for natural human weakness. While selfish, he was not self-conscious, and it never occurred to him, it was impossible for him to see that he was a giant among men. His heart was callous; his whole nature and character hard and flinty from the buffetings he gave rather than received.

Then had come misfortune. Ferriss had died, and Bennett's recognition and acknowledgment of the fact that he, Ward Bennett, who never failed, who never blundered, had made at last the great and terrible error of his life, had shaken his character to its very foundations. This was only the beginning; the breach once made, Humanity entered into the gloomy, waste places of his soul; remorse crowded hard upon his wonted arrogance; generosity and the impulse to make amends took the place of selfishness; kindness thrust out the native brutality; the old-time harshness and imperiousness gave way to a certain spirit of toleration.

It was the influence of these new emotions that had moved Bennett to make the statement to Adler that had so astonished and perplexed his old-time subordinate. He, Bennett, too, like Lloyd, was at that time endeavouring to free himself from a false position, and through the medium of confession stand in his true colours in the eyes of his associates. Unconsciously they were both working out their salvation along the same lines.

Then had come Bennett's resolve to give Ferriss the conspicuous and prominent place in his book, the account of the expedition. The more Bennett dwelt upon Ferriss's heroism, intelligence, and ability the more his task became a labour of love, and the more the idea of self dropped away from his thought and imagination. Then—and perhaps this was not the least important factor in Bennett's transformation—sickness had befallen; the strong and self-reliant man had been brought to the weakness of a child, whom the pressure of a finger could control. He suddenly changed places with the woman he believed he had, at such fearful cost, broken and subdued. His physical strength, once so enormous, was as a reed in the woman's hand; his will, so indomitable, was as powerless as an infant's before the woman's calm resolve, rising up there before him and overmastering him at a time he believed it to be forever weakened.

Bennett had come forth from the ordeal chastened, softened, and humbled. But he was shattered, broken, brought to the earth with sorrow and the load of unavailing regret. Ambition was numb and lifeless within him. Reaction from his former attitude of aggression and defiance had carried him far beyond the normal.

Here widened the difference between the man and the woman. Lloyd's discontinuance of her life-work had been in the nature of heroic subjugation of self. Bennett's abandonment of his career was hardly better than weakness. In the one it had been renunciation; in the other surrender. In the end, and after all was over, it was the woman who remained the stronger.

But for her, the woman, was it true that all was over? Had the last conflict been fought? Was it not rather to be believed that life was one long conflict? Was it not for her, Lloyd, to rouse that sluggard ambition? Was not this her career, after all, to be his inspiration, his incentive, to urge him to the accomplishment of a great work? Now, of the two, she was the stronger. In these new conditions what was her duty? Adler's clumsy phrases persisted in her mind. "That's his work," Adler had said. "God Almighty cut him out for that, and he's got to do it. Don't let him chuck, don't let him get soft; make him be a man and not a professor."

Had she so much influence over Bennett? Could she rouse the restless, daring spirit again? Perhaps; but what would it mean for her—for her, who must be left behind to wait, and wait, and wait —for three years, for five years, for ten years—perhaps forever? And now, at this moment, when she believed that at last happiness had come to her; when the duty had been done, the grim problems solved; when sickness had been overcome; when love had come back, and the calm, untroubled days seemed lengthening out ahead, there came to her recollection the hideous lapse of time that had intervened between the departure of the Freja and the expedition's return; what sleepless nights, what

days of unspeakable suspense, what dreadful alter-
nations between hope and despair, what silent, re-
pressed suffering, what haunting, ever-present dread
of a thing she dared not name! Was the Fear to
come into her life again; the Enemy that lurked and
leered and forebore to strike, that hung upon her
heels at every hour of the day, that sat down with
her to her every occupation, that followed after
when she stirred abroad, that came close to her in
the still watches of the night, creeping, creeping to
her bedside, looming over her in the darkness; the
cold fingers reaching closer and closer, the awful
face growing ever more distinct, till the suspense
of waiting for the blow to fall, for the fingers to grip,
became more than she could bear, and she sprang
from her bed with a stifled sob of anguish, driven
from her rest with quivering lips and streaming
eyes?

Abruptly Lloyd rose to her feet, the flowers falling unheeded from her lap, her arms rigid at her
side, her hands shut tight.

"No," she murmured, "I cannot. This, at last,
is more than I can do."

Instantly Adler's halting words went ringing
through her brain: "The danger don't figure;
nothing in the world don't figure. It's his work."

Adler's words were the words of the world. She
alone of the thousands whose eyes were turned
toward Bennett was blinded. She was wrong.
She belonged to him, but he did not belong to her.
The world demanded him; the world called him
from her side to do the terrible work that God had
made him for. Was she, because she loved him,

because of her own single anguish, to stand between him and the clamour of the world, between him and his work, between him and God?

A work there was for him to do. He must play the man's part. The battle must be fought again. That horrible, grisly Enemy far up there to the north, upon the high curve of the globe, the shoulder of the world, huge, remorseless, terrible in its vast, Titanic strength, guarding its secret through all the centuries in the innermost of a thousand gleaming coils, must be defied again. The monster that defended the great prize, the object of so many fruitless quests must be once more attacked.

His was the work, for him the shock of battle, the rigour of the fight, the fierce assault, the ceaseless onset, the unfailing and unflinching courage.

Hers was the woman's part. Already she had assumed it; steadfast unselfishness, renunciation, patience, the heroism greater than all others, that sits with folded hands, quiet, unshaken, and under fearful stress, endures, and endures, and endures. To be the inspiration of great deeds, high hopes, and firm resolves, and then, while the fight was dared, to wait in calmness for its issue—that was her duty; that, the woman's part in the world's great work.

Lloyd was dimly conscious of a certain sweet and subtle element in her love for Bennett that only of late she had begun to recognise and be aware of. This was a certain vague protective, almost maternal, instinct. Perhaps it was because of his present weakness both of body and character, or perhaps it was an element always to be found in the deep and earnest love of any noble-hearted woman. She felt that she, not as herself individually, but as a woman, was not only stronger than Bennett, but in a manner older, more mature. She was conscious of depths in her nature far greater than in his, and also that she was capable of attaining heights of heroism, devotion, and sacrifice which he, for all his masculine force, could not only never reach, but could not even conceive of. It was this consciousness of her larger, better nature that made her feel for Bennett somewhat as a mother feels for a son, a sister for her younger brother. A great tenderness mingled with her affection, a vast and almost divine magnanimity, a broad, womanly pity for his shortcomings, his errors, his faults. It was to her he must look for encouragement. It was for her to bind up and reshape the great energy that had been so rudely checked, and not only to call back his strength, but to guide it and direct into its appointed channels.

Lloyd returned toward the glass-enclosed veranda to find Bennett just arousing from his nap. She drew the shawls closer about him and rearranged the pillows under his head, and then sat down on the steps near at hand.

" Tell me about this Captain Duane," she began. " Where is he now? "

Bennett yawned and passed his hand across his face, rubbing the sleep from his eyes.

" What time is it? I must have slept over an hour. Duane? Why, you saw what the paper said. I presume he is at Tasiusak."

" Do you think he will succeed? Do you think he will reach the Pole? Adler thinks he won't."

"Oh, perhaps, if he has luck and an open season."

"But tell me, why does he take so many men? Isn't that contrary to the custom? I know a great deal about arctic work. While you were away I read every book I could get upon the subject. The best work has been done with small expeditions. If you should go again—when you go again, will you take so many? I saw you quoted somewhere as being in favour of only six or eight men."

"Ten should be the limit—but some one else will make the attempt now. I'm out of it. I tried and failed."

"Failed—you! The idea of you ever failing, of you ever giving up! Of course it was all very well to joke this morning about giving up your career; but I know you will be up and away again only too soon. I am trying to school myself to expect that."

"Lloyd, I tell you that I am out of it. I don't believe the Pole ever can be reached, and I don't much care whether it is reached or not."

Suddenly Lloyd turned to him, the unwonted light flashing in her eyes. "*I* do, though," she cried vehemently. "It can be done, and we— America—ought to do it."

Bennett stared at her, startled by her outburst.

"This English expedition," Lloyd continued, the colour flushing in her cheeks, "this Duane-Parsons expedition, they will have the start of everybody next year. Nearly every attempt that is made now establishes a new record for a high latitude. One nation after another is creeping nearer and nearer almost every year, and each expedition is profiting by the experiences and observations made by the one that preceded it. Some day, and not very long now, some nation is going to succeed and plant its flag there at last. Why should it not be us? Why shouldn't *our* flag be first at the Pole? We who have had so many heroes, such great sailors, such splendid leaders, such explorers—our Stanleys, our Farraguts, our Decaturs, our De Longs, our Lockwoods—how we would stand ashamed before the world if some other nation should succeed where we have all but succeeded—Norway, or France, or Russia, or England—profiting by our experiences, following where we have made the way!"

"That is very fine," admitted Bennett. "It would be a great honour, the greatest perhaps; and once—I—well, I had my ambitions, too. But it's all different now. Something in me died when—Dick—when—I—oh, let Duane try. Let him do his best. I know it can't be done, and if he should win, I would be the first to wire congratulations. Lloyd, I don't care. I've lost interest. I suppose it is my punishment. I'm out of the race. I'm a back number. I'm down."

Lloyd shook her head.

"I don't—I can't believe you."

"Do you want to see me go," demanded Bennett, "after this last experience? Do you urge me to it?"

Lloyd turned her head away, leaning it against one of the veranda pillars. A sudden dimness swam in her eyes, the choking ache she knew so well came to her throat. Ah, life was hard for her. The very greatness of her nature drove from her the happiness so constantly attained by little minds, by commonplace souls. When was it to end, this continual sacrifice of inclination to duty, this eternal abnegation, this yielding up of herself, her dearest, most cherished wishes to the demands of duty and the great world?

"I don't know what I want," she said faintly. "It don't seem as if one *could* be happy—very long."

All at once she moved close to him and laid her cheek upon the arm of his chair and clasped his hand in both her own, murmuring: "But I have you now, I have you now, no matter what is coming to us."

A sense of weakness overcame her. What did she care that Bennett should fulfil his destiny, should round out his career, should continue to be the Great Man? It was he, Bennett, that she loved— not his greatness, not his career. Let it all go, let ambition die, let others less worthy succeed in the mighty task. What were fame and honour and glory and the sense of a divinely appointed duty done at last to the clasp of his hand and the sound of his voice?

In November of that year Lloyd and Bennett were married. Two guests only assisted at the ceremony. These were Campbell and his little daughter Hattie.

X.

The months passed; Christmas came and went. Until then the winter had been unusually mild, but January set in with a succession of vicious cold snaps and great blustering winds out of the northeast. Lloyd and Bennett had elected to remain quietly in their new home at Medford. They had no desire to travel, and Bennett's forthcoming book demanded his attention. Adler stayed on about the house. He and the dog Kamiska were companions inseparable. At long intervals visitors presented themselves—Dr. Street, or Pitts, or certain friends of Bennett's. But the great rush of interviewers, editors, and projectors of marvellous schemes that had crowded Bennett's anterooms during the spring and early summer was conspicuously dwindling. The press ceased to speak of him; even his mail had fallen away. Now, whenever the journals of the day devoted space to arctic exploration, it was invariably in reference to the English expedition wintering on the Greenland coast. That world that had clamoured so loudly upon Bennett's return, while, perhaps, not yet forgetting him, was already ignoring him, was looking in other directions. Another man was in the public eye.

But in every sense these two—Lloyd and Bennett —were out of the world. They had freed themselves from the current of affairs. They stood aside while the great tide went careering past swift and turbulent, and one of them at least lacked even the interest to look on and watch its progress.

For a time Lloyd was supremely happy. Their life was unbroken, uneventful. The calm, monotonous days of undisturbed happiness to which she had looked forward were come at last. Thus it was always to be. Isolated and apart, she could shut her ears to the thunder of the world's great tide that somewhere, off beyond the hills in the direction of the City, went swirling through its channels. Hardly an hour went by that she and Bennett were not together. Lloyd had transferred her stable to her new home; Lewis was added to the number of their servants, and until Bennett's old-time vigour completely returned to him she drove out almost daily with her husband, covering the country for miles around.

Much of their time, however, they spent in Bennett's study. This was a great apartment in the rear of the house, scantily, almost meanly, furnished. Papers littered the floor; bundles of manuscripts, lists, charts, and observations, the worn and battered tin box of records, note-books, journals, tables of logarithms were piled upon Bennett's desk. A bookcase crammed with volumes of reference, statistical pamphlets, and the like stood between the windows, while one of the walls was nearly entirely occupied by a vast map of the arctic circle, upon which the course of the Freja, her drift in the pack, and the route of the expedition's southerly march were accurately plotted.

The room was bare of ornament; the desk and a

couple of chairs were its only furniture. Pictures there were none. Their places were taken by photographs and a great blue print of the shipbuilder's plans and specifications of the Freja.

The photographs were some of those that Dennison had made of the expedition—the Freja nipped in the ice, a group of the officers and crew upon the forward deck, the coast of Wrangel Island, Cape Kammeni, peculiar ice formations, views of the pack under different conditions and temperatures, pressure-ridges and scenes of the expedition's daily life in the arctic, bear-hunts, the manufacture of sledges, dog-teams, Bennett taking soundings and reading the wind-gauge, and one, the last view of the Freja, taken just as the ship—her ice-sheathed dripping bows heaved high in the air, the flag still at the peak—sank from sight.

However, on the wall over the blue-print plans of the Freja, one of the boat's flags, that had been used by the expedition throughout all the time of its stay in the ice, hung suspended—a faded, tattered square of stars and bars.

As the new life settled quietly and evenly to its grooves a routine began to develop. About an hour after breakfast Lloyd and Bennett shut themselves in Bennett's "workroom," as he called it, Lloyd taking her place at the desk. She had become his amanuensis, had insisted upon writing to his dictation.

"Look at that manuscript," she had exclaimed one day, turning the sheets that Bennett had written; "literally the very worst handwriting I have ever seen. What do you suppose a printer would make out of your 'thes' and 'ands'? It's hieroglyphics, you know," she informed him gravely, nodding her head at him.

It was quite true. Bennett wrote with amazing rapidity and with ragged, vigorous strokes of the pen, not unfrequently driving the point through the paper itself; his script was pothooks, clumsy, slanting in all directions, all but illegible. In the end Lloyd had almost pushed him from his place at the desk, taking the pen from between his fingers, exclaiming:

"Get up! Give me your chair—and that pen. Handwriting like that is nothing else but a sin."

Bennett allowed her to bully him, protesting merely for the enjoyment of squabbling with her.

"Come, I like this. What are you doing in my workroom anyhow, Mrs. Bennett? I think you had better go to your housework."

"Don't talk," she answered. "Here are your notes and journal. Now tell me what to write."

In the end matters adjusted themselves. Daily Lloyd took her place at the desk, pen in hand, the sleeve of her right arm rolled back to the elbow (a habit of hers whenever writing, and which Bennett found to be charming beyond words), her pen travelling steadily from line to line. He on his part paced the floor, a cigar between his teeth, his notes and note-books in his hand, dictating comments of his own, or quoting from the pages, stained, frayed, and crumpled, written by the light of the auroras, the midnight suns, or the unsteady, flickering of train-oil lanterns and blubber-lamps.

What long, delicious hours they spent thus, as the

winter drew on, in the absolute quiet of that country house, ignored and lost in the brown, bare fields and leafless orchards of the open country! No one troubled them. No one came near them. They asked nothing better than that the world wherein they once had lived, whose hurtling activity and febrile unrest they both had known so well, should leave them alone.

Only one jarring note, and that none too resonant, broke the long harmony of Lloyd's happiness during these days. Bennett was deaf to it; but for Lloyd it vibrated continuously and, as time passed, with increasing insistence and distinctness. But for one person in the world Lloyd could have told herself that her life was without a single element of discontent.

This was Adler. It was not that his presence about the house was a reproach to Bennett's wife, for the man was scrupulously unobtrusive. He had the instinctive delicacy that one sometimes discovers in simple, undeveloped natures—seafaring folk especially—and though he could not bring himself to leave his former chief, he had withdrawn himself more than ever from notice since the time of Bennett's marriage. He rarely even waited on the table these days, for Lloyd and Bennett often chose to breakfast and dine quite to themselves.

But, for all that, Lloyd saw Adler from time to time, Kamiska invariably at his heels. She came upon him polishing the brasses upon the door of the house, or binding strips of burlaps and sacking about the rose-bushes in the garden, or returning from the village post-office with the mail, invariably wearing the same woollen cap, the old pea-jacket, and the jersey with the name "Freja" upon the breast. He rarely spoke to her unless she first addressed him, and then always with a precise salute, bringing his heels sharply together, standing stiffly at attention.

But the man, though all unwittingly, radiated gloom. Lloyd readily saw that Adler was labouring under a certain cloud of disappointment and deferred hope. Naturally she understood the cause. Lloyd was too large-hearted to feel any irritation at the sight of Adler. But she could not regard him with indifference. To her mind he stood for all that Bennett had given up, for the great career that had stopped half-way, for the work half done, the task only half completed. In a way was not Adler now superior to Bennett? His one thought and aim and hope was to "try again." His ambition was yet alive and alight; the soldier was willing where the chief lost heart. Never again had Adler addressed himself to Lloyd on the subject of Bennett's inactivity. Now he seemed to understand—to realise that once married—and to Lloyd—he must no longer expect Bennett to continue the work. All this Lloyd interpreted from Adler's attitude, and again and again told herself that she could read the man's thoughts aright. She even fancied she caught a mute appeal in his eyes upon those rare occasions when they met, as though he looked to her as the only hope, the only means to wake Bennett from his lethargy. She imagined that she heard him say:

"Ain't you got any influence with him, Miss?

A Man's Woman

Won't you talk good talk to him? Don't let him chuck. Make him be a man, and not a professor. Nothing else in the world don't figure. It's his work. God A'mighty cut him out for that, and he's got to do it."

His work, his work, God made him for that; appointed the task, made the man, and now she came between. God, Man, and the Work,—the three vast elements of an entire system, the whole universe epitomised in the tremendous trinity. Again and again such thoughts assailed her. Duty once more stirred and awoke. It seemed to her as if some great engine ordained of Heaven to run its appointed course had come to a standstill, was rusting to its ruin, and that she alone of all the world had power to grasp its lever, to send it on its way; whither, she did not know; why, she could not tell. She knew only that it was right that she should act. By degrees her resolution hardened. Bennett must try again. But at first it seemed to her as though her heart would break, and more than once she wavered.

As Bennett continued to dictate to her the story of the expedition he arrived at the account of the march toward Kolyuchin Bay, and, finally, at the description of the last week, with its terrors, its sufferings, its starvation, its despair, when, one by one, the men died in their sleeping-bags, to be buried under slabs of ice. When this point in the narrative was reached Bennett inserted no comment of his own; but while Lloyd wrote, read simply and with grim directness from the entries in his journal precisely as they had been written.

A Man's Woman

Lloyd had known in a vague way that the expedition had suffered abominably, but hitherto Bennett had never consented to tell her the story in detail. "It was a hard week," he informed her, "a rather bad grind."

Now, for the first time, she was to know just what had happened, just what he had endured.

As usual, Bennett paced the floor from wall to wall, his cigar in his teeth, his tattered, grimy ice-journal in his hand. At the desk Lloyd's round, bare arm, the sleeve turned up to the elbow, moved evenly back and forth as she wrote. In the intervals of Bennett's dictation the scratching of Lloyd's pen made itself heard. A little fire snapped and crackled on the hearth. The morning's sun came flooding in at the windows.

". . . Gale of wind from the northeast," prompted Lloyd, raising her head from her writing. Bennett continued:

Impossible to march against it in our weakened condition.

He paused for her to complete the sentence.

. . . Must camp here till it abates. . . .

"Have you got that?" Lloyd nodded.

. . . Made soup of the last of the dog-meat this afternoon. . . . Our last pemmican gone.

There was a pause; then Bennett resumed:

December 1st, Wednesday—Everybody getting weaker. . . . Metz breaking down. . . . Sent Adler to the shore to gather shrimps; . . . we had about a mouthful apiece at noon;   . . .   supper, a spoonful of glycerine and hot water.

Lloyd put her hand to her temple, smoothing back her hair, her face turned away. As before, in the park, on that warm and glowing summer afternoon, a swift, clear vision of the Ice was vouchsafed to her. She saw the coast of Kolyuchin Bay—primordial desolation, whirling dust-like snow, the unleashed wind yelling like a sabbath of witches, leaping and somersaulting from rock to rock, folly-stricken and insensate in its hideous dance of death. Bennett continued. His voice insensibly lowered itself, a certain gravity of manner came upon him. At times he looked at the written pages in his hand with vague, unseeing eyes. No doubt he, too, was remembering.

He resumed:

December 2d, Thursday—Metz died during the night. . . . Hansen dying. Still blowing a gale from the northeast. . . . A hard night.

Lloyd's pen moved slower and slower as she wrote. The lines of the manuscript began to blur and swim before her eyes.

And it was to this that she must send him. To this inhuman, horrible region; to this life of prolonged suffering, where death came slowly through days of starvation, exhaustion, and agony hourly renewed. He must dare it all again. She must force him to it. Her decision had been taken; her duty was plain to her. Now it was irrevocable.

. . . Hansen died during early morning. . . . Dennison breaking down. . . .

A Man's Woman

. . . December 5th—Sunday—Dennison found dead this morning between Adler and myself. . . .

The vision became plainer, more distinct. She fancied she saw the interior of the tent and the dwindling number of the Freja's survivors moving about on their hands and knees in its gloomy half-light. Their hair and beards were long, their faces black with dirt, monstrously distended and fat with the bloated irony of starvation. They were no longer men. After that unspeakable stress of misery nothing but the animal remained.

. . . Too weak to bury him, or even carry him out of the tent. . . . He must lie where he is. . . . Last spoonful of glycerine and hot water. . . . Divine service at 5:30 P.M. . . .

Once more Lloyd faltered in her writing; her hand moved slower. Shut her teeth though she might, the sobs would come; swiftly the tears brimmed her eyes, but she tried to wink them back, lest Bennett should see. Heroically she wrote to the end of the sentence. A pause followed:

" Yes—' divine services at '—I—I——"

The pen dropped from her fingers and she sank down upon her desk, her head bowed in the hollow of her bare arm, shaken from head to foot with the violence of the cruelest grief she had ever known. Bennett threw his journal from him, and came to her, taking her in his arms, putting her head upon his shoulder.

" Why, Lloyd, what is it—why, old chap what the devil ! I was a beast to read that to you. It wasn't really as bad as that, you know, and besides, look here, look at me. It all happened three years ago. It's all over with now."

Without raising her head, and clinging to him all the closer, Lloyd answered brokenly:

" No, no; it's not all over. It never, never will be."

" Pshaw, nonsense!" Bennett blustered, " you must not take it to heart like this. We're going to forget all about it now. Here, damn the book, anyhow! We've had enough of it to-day. Put your hat on. We'll have the ponies out and drive somewhere. And to-night we'll go into town and see a show at a theatre."

" No," protested Lloyd, pushing back from him, drying her eyes. " You shall not think I'm so weak. We will go on with what we have to do—with our work. I'm all right now."

Bennett marched her out of the room without more ado, and, following her, closed and locked the door behind them. " We'll not write another word of that stuff to-day. Get your hat and things. I'm going out to tell Lewis to put the ponies in."

But that day marked a beginning. From that time on Lloyd never faltered, and if there were moments when the iron bit deeper than usual into her heart, Bennett never knew her pain. By degrees a course of action planned itself for her. A direct appeal to Bennett she believed would not only be useless, but beyond even her heroic courage. She must influence him indirectly. The initiative must appear to come from him. It must seem to him that he, of his own accord, roused his dormant resolution. It was a situation that called for all her feminine tact, all her delicacy, all her instinctive diplomacy.

The round of their daily life was renewed, but now there was a change. It was subtle, illusive, a vague, indefinite trouble in the air. Lloyd had addressed herself to her task, and from day to day, from hour to hour, she held to it, unseen, unnoticed. Now it was a remark dropped as if by chance in the course of conversation; now an extract cut from a newspaper or scientific journal, and left where Bennett would find it; now merely a look in her eyes, an instant's significant glance when her gaze met her husband's, or a moment's enthusiasm over the news of some discovery. Insensibly and with infinite caution she directed his attention to the world he believed he had abjured; she called into being his interest in his own field of action, reading to him by the hour from the writings of other men, or advancing and championing theories which she knew to be false and ridiculous, but which she goaded him to deny and refute.

One morning she even feigned an exclamation of unbounded astonishment as she opened the newspaper while the two were at breakfast, pretending to read from imaginary headlines.

"Ward, listen! 'The Pole at Last. A Norwegian Expedition Solves the Mystery of the Arctic. The Goal Reached After——'"

"What!" cried Bennett sharply, his frown lowering.

"'——After Centuries of Failure.'" Lloyd put down the paper with a note of laughter.

A Man's Woman

"Suppose you should read it some day."

Bennett subsided with a good-humoured growl.

"You did scare me for a moment. I thought—I thought——"

"I did scare you? Why were you scared? What did you think?" She leaned toward him eagerly.

"I thought—well—oh—that some other chap, Duane, perhaps——"

"He's still at Tasiusak. But he will succeed, I do believe. I've read a great deal about him. He has energy and determination. If anybody succeeds it will be Duane."

"He? Never!"

"Somebody, then."

"You said once that if your husband couldn't nobody could."

"Yes, yes, I know," she answered cheerfully. "But you—you are out of it now."

"Huh!" he grumbled. "It's not because I don't think I could if I wanted to."

"No, you could not, Ward. Nobody can."

"But you just said you thought somebody would some day."

"Did I? Oh, suppose you really should one of these days!"

"And suppose I never came back?"

"Nonsense! Of course you would come back. They all do nowadays."

"De Long didn't."

"But you are not De Long."

And for the rest of the day Lloyd noted with a sinking heart that Bennett was unusually thoughtful and preoccupied. She said nothing, and was studious to avoid breaking in upon his reflections, whatever they might be. She kept out of his way as much as possible, but left upon his desk, as if by accident, a copy of a pamphlet issued by a geographical society, open at an article upon the future of exploration within the arctic circle. At supper that night Bennett suddenly broke in upon a rather prolonged silence with:

"It's all in the ship. Build a ship strong enough to withstand lateral pressure of the ice and the whole thing becomes easy."

Lloyd yawned and stirred her tea indifferently as she answered:

"Yes, but you know that can't be done."

Bennett frowned thoughtfully, drumming upon the table.

"I'll wager *I* could build one."

"But it's not the ship alone. It's the man. Whom would you get to command your ship?"

Bennett stared.

"Why, I would take her, of course."

"You? You have had your share—your chance. Now you can afford to stay home and finish your book—and—well, you might deliver lectures."

"What rot, Lloyd! Can you see me posing on a lecture platform?"

"I would rather see you doing that than trying to beat Duane, than getting into the ice again. I would rather see you doing that than to know that you were away up there—in the north, in the ice, at your work again, fighting your way toward the Pole, leading your men and overcoming every obstacle that stood in your way, never giving up, never losing heart, trying to do the great, splendid, impossible thing; risking your life to reach merely a point on a chart. Yes, I would rather see you on a lecture platform than on the deck of an arctic steamship. You know that, Ward."

He shot a glance at her.

" I would like to know what you mean," he muttered.

The winter went by, then the spring, and by June all the country around Medford was royal with summer. During the last days of May, Bennett practically had completed the body of his book and now occupied himself with its appendix. There was little variation in their daily life. Adler became more and more of a fixture about the place. In the first week of June, Lloyd and Bennett had a visitor, a guest; this was Hattie Campbell. Mr. Campbell was away upon a business trip, and Lloyd had arranged to have the little girl spend the fortnight of his absence with her at Medford.

The summer was delightful. A vast, pervading warmth lay close over all the world. The trees, the orchards, the rose-bushes in the garden about the house, all the teeming life of trees and plants hung motionless and poised in the still, tideless ocean of the air. It was very quiet; all distant noises, the crowing of cocks, the persistent calling of robins and jays, the sound of wheels upon the road, the rumble of the trains passing the station down in the town, seemed muffled and subdued. The long, calm summer days succeeded one another in an unbroken, glimmering procession. From dawn to twilight

one heard the faint, innumerable murmurs of the
summer, the dull bourdon of bees in the rose and
lilac bushes, the prolonged, strident buzzing of blue-
bottle-flies, the harsh, dry scrape of grasshoppers,
the stridulating of an occasional cricket. In the
twilight and all through the night itself the frogs
shrilled from the hedgerows and in the damp, north
corners of the fields, while from the direction of the
hills toward the east the whippoorwills called incessantly. During the day the air was full of odours,
distilled as it were by the heat of high noon—the
sweet smell of ripening apples, the fragrance of
warm sap and leaves and growing grass, the smell
of cows from the nearby pastures, the pungent, am-
moniacal suggestion of the stable back of the house,
and the odour of scorching paint blistering on the
southern walls.

July was very hot. No breath of wind stirred the
vast, invisible sea of air, quivering and oily under
the vertical sun. The landscape was deserted of
animated life; there was little stirring abroad. In
the house one kept within the cool, darkened rooms
with matting on the floors and comfortable, deep
wicker chairs, the windows wide to the least stirring
of the breeze. Adler dozed in his canvas hammock
slung between a hitching-post and a crab-apple tree
in the shade behind the stable. Kamiska sprawled
at full length underneath the water-trough, her
tongue lolling, panting incessantly. An immeas-
urable Sunday stillness seemed to hang suspended in
the atmosphere—a drowsy, numbing hush. There
was no thought of the passing of time. The day of
the week was always a matter of conjecture. It

seemed as though this life of heat and quiet and unbroken silence was to last forever.

Then suddenly there was an *alerte*. One morning, a day or so after Hattie Campbell had returned to the City, just as Lloyd and Bennett were finishing their breakfast in the now heavily awninged glass-room, they were surprised to see Adler running down the road toward the house, Kamiska racing on ahead, barking excitedly. Adler had gone into the town for the mail and morning's paper. This latter he held wide open in his hand, and as soon as he caught sight of Lloyd and Bennett waved it about him, shouting as he ran.

Lloyd's heart began to beat. There was only one thing that could excite Adler to this degree—the English expedition; Adler had news of it; it was in the paper. Duane had succeeded; had been working steadily northward during all these past months, while Bennett——

"Stuck in the ice! stuck in the ice!" shouted Adler as he swung wide the front gate and came hastening toward the veranda across the lawn. "What did we say! Hooray! He's stuck. I knew it; any galoot might 'a' known it. Duane's stuck tighter 'n a wedge off Bache Island, in Kane Basin. Here it all is; read it for yourself."

Bennett took the paper from him and read aloud to the effect that the Curlew, accompanied by her collier, which was to follow her to the southerly limit of Kane Basin, had attempted the passage of Smith Sound late in June. But the season, as had been feared, was late. The enormous quantities of ice reported by the whalers the previous year had not debouched from the narrow channel, and on the last day of June the Curlew had found her further progress effectually blocked.   In essaying to force her way into a lead the ice had closed in behind her, and, while not as yet nipped, the vessel was immobilised.   There was no hope that she would advance northward until the following summer.   The collier, which had not been beset, had returned to Tasiusak with the news of the failure.

"What a galoot!   What a—a professor!" exclaimed Adler with a vast disdain.   "Him loafing at Tasiusak waiting for open water, when the Alert wintered in eighty-two-twenty-four!   Well, he's shelved for another year, anyhow."

Later on, after breakfast, Lloyd and Bennett shut themselves in Bennett's workroom, and for upward of three hours addressed themselves to the unfinished work of the previous day, compiling from Bennett's notes a table of temperatures of the seawater taken at different soundings.   Alternating with the scratching of Lloyd's pen, Bennett's voice continued monotonously:

August 15th—2,000 meters or 1,093 fathoms—minus .66 degrees centigrade or 30.81 Fahrenheit.

"Fahrenheit," repeated Lloyd as she wrote the last word.

August 16th—1,600 meters or 874 fathoms——

"Eight hundred and seventy-four fathoms," repeated Lloyd as Bennett paused abstractedly.

"Or . . . he's in a bad way, you know."

"What do you mean?"

"It's a bad bit of navigation along there. The
Proteus was nipped and crushed to kindling in
about that same latitude . . . h'm " . . .
Bennett tugged at his mustache. Then, suddenly,
as if coming to himself : " Well—these temperatures now. Where were we? 'Eight hundred and
seventy-four fathoms, minus forty-six hundredths
degrees centigrade.' "

On the afternoon of the next day, just as they
were finishing this table, there was a knock at the
door. It was Adler, and as Bennett opened the
door he saluted and handed him three calling-cards.
Bennett uttered an exclamation of surprise, and
Lloyd turned about from the desk, her pen poised
in the air over the half-written sheet.

"They might have let me know they were coming," she heard Bennett mutter. "What do they
want?"

"Guess they came on that noon train, sir," hazarded Adler. "They didn't say what they wanted,
just inquired for you."

"Who is it?" asked Lloyd, coming forward.

Bennett read off the names on the cards.

"Well, it's Tremlidge—that's the Tremlidge of
the Times; he's the editor and proprietor—and
Hamilton Garlock—has something to do with that
new geographical society—president, I believe—and
this one "—he handed her the third card—" is a
friend of yours, Craig V. Campbell, of the Hercules
Wrought Steel Company."

Lloyd stared. "What can they want?" she murmured, looking up to him from the card in some
perplexity. Bennett shook his head.

"Tell them to come up here," he said to Adler.

Lloyd hastily drew down her sleeve over her bare arm.

"Why up here, Ward?" she inquired abruptly.

"Should we have seen them downstairs?" he demanded with a frown. "I suppose so; I didn't think. Don't go," he added, putting a hand on her arm as she started for the door. "You might as well hear what they have to say."

The visitors entered, Adler holding open the door —Campbell, well groomed, clean-shaven, and gloved even in that warm weather; Tremlidge, the editor of one of the greater daily papers of the City (and of the country for the matter of that), who wore a monocle and carried a straw hat under his arm; and Garlock, the vice-president of an international geographical society, an old man, with beautiful white hair curling about his ears, a great bow of black silk knotted about his old-fashioned collar. The group presented, all unconsciously, three great and highly developed phases of nineteenth-century intelligence—science, manufactures, and journalism—each man of them a master in his calling.

When the introductions and preliminaries were over, Bennett took up his position again in front of the fireplace, leaning against the mantle, his hands in his pockets. Lloyd sat opposite to him at the desk, resting her elbow on the edge. Hanging against the wall behind her was the vast chart of the arctic circle. Tremlidge, the editor, sat on the bamboo sofa near the end of the room, his elbows on his knees, gently tapping the floor with the fer-

rule of his slim walking-stick; Garlock, the scientist,
had dropped into the depths of a huge leather chair
and leaned back in it comfortably, his legs crossed,
one boot swinging gently; Campbell stood behind
this chair, drumming on the back occasionally with
the fingers of one hand, speaking to Bennett over
Garlock's shoulder, and from time to time turning
to Tremlidge for corroboration and support of what
he was saying.

Abruptly the conference began.

"Well, Mr. Bennett, you got our wire?" Campbell said by way of commencement.

Bennett shook his head.

"No," he returned in some surprise; "no, I got
no wire."

"That's strange," said Tremlidge. "I wired
three days ago asking for this interview. The address was right, I think. I wired: 'Care of Dr.
Pitts.' Isn't that right?"

"That probably accounts for it," answered Bennett. "This is Pitts's house, but he does not live
here now. Your despatch, no doubt, went to his
office in the City, and was forwarded to him. He's
away just now, travelling, I believe. But—you're
here. That's the essential."

"Yes," murmured Garlock, looking to Campbell.
"We're here, and we want to have a talk with you."

Campbell, who had evidently been chosen spokesman, cleared his throat.

"Well, Mr. Bennett, I don't know just how to
begin, so suppose I begin at the beginning. Tremlidge and I belong to the same club in the City, and
in some way or other we have managed to see a

good deal of each other during the last half-dozen years. We find that we have a good deal in common. I don't think his editorial columns are for sale, and he doesn't believe there are blow-holes in my steel plates. I really do believe we have certain convictions. Tremlidge seems to have an idea that journalism can be clean and yet enterprising, and tries to run his sheet accordingly, and I am afraid that I would not make a bid for bridge girders below what it would cost to manufacture them honestly. Tremlidge and I differ in politics; we hold conflicting views as to municipal government; we attend different churches; we are at variance in the matter of public education, of the tariff, of emigration, and, heaven save the mark! of capital and labour, but we tell ourselves that we are public-spirited and are a little proud that God allowed us to be born in the United States; also it appears that we have more money than Henry George believes to be right. Now," continued Mr. Campbell, straightening himself as though he were about to touch upon the real subject of his talk, " when the news of your return, Mr. Bennett, was received, it was, as of course you understand, the one topic of conversation in the streets, the clubs, the newspaper offices—everywhere. Tremlidge and I met at our club at luncheon the next week, and I remember perfectly well how long and how very earnestly we talked of your work and of arctic exploration in general.

" We found out all of a sudden that here at last was a subject we were agreed upon, a subject in which we took an extraordinary mutual interest. We discovered that we had read almost every explorer's book from Sir John Franklin down. We knew all about the different theories and plans of reaching the Pole. We knew how and why they had all failed; but, for all that, we were both of the opinion " (Campbell leaned forward, speaking with considerable energy) " that it can be done, and that America ought to do it. That would be something better than even a World's Fair.

" We give out a good deal of money, Tremlidge and I, every year to public works and one thing or another. We buy pictures by American artists—pictures that we don't want; we found a scholarship now and then; we contribute money to build groups of statuary in the park; we give checks to the finance committees of libraries and museums and all the rest of it, but, for the lives of us, we can feel only a mild interest in the pictures and statues, and museums and colleges, though we go on buying the one and supporting the other, because we think that somehow it is right for us to do it. I'm afraid we are men more of action than of art, literature, and the like. Tremlidge is, I know. He wants facts, accomplished results. When he gives out his money he wants to see the concrete, substantial return—and I'm not sure that I am not of the same way of thinking.

" Well, with this and with that, and after talking it all over a dozen times—twenty times—we came to the conclusion that what we would most like to aid financially would be a successful attempt by an American-built ship, manned by American seamen, led by an American commander, to reach the North Pole. We came to be very enthusiastic about our idea; but we want it American from start to finish. We will start the subscription, and want to head the list with our checks; but we want every bolt in that ship forged in American foundries from metal dug out of American soil. We want every plank in her hull shaped from American trees, every sail of her woven by American looms, every man of her born of American parents, and we want it this way because we believe in American manufactures, because we believe in American shipbuilding, because we believe in American sailmakers, and because we believe in the intelligence and pluck and endurance and courage of the American sailor.

" Well," Campbell continued, changing his position and speaking in a quieter voice, " we did not say much to anybody, and, in fact, we never really planned any expedition at all. We merely talked about its practical nature and the desirability of having it distinctively American. This was all last summer. What we wanted to do was to make the scheme a popular one. It would not be hard to raise a hundred thousand dollars from among a dozen or so men whom we both know, and we found that we could count upon the financial support of Mr. Garlock's society. That was all very well, but we wanted the *people* to back this enterprise. We would rather get a thousand five-dollar subscriptions than five of a thousand dollars each. When our ship went out we wanted her commander to feel, not that there were merely a few millionaires, who had paid for his equipment and his vessel, behind him, but that he had seventy millions of people, a whole nation, at his back.

"So Tremlidge went to work and telegraphed instructions to the Washington correspondents of his paper to sound quietly the temper of as many Congressmen as possible in the matter of making an appropriation toward such an expedition. It was not so much the money we wanted as the sanction of the United States. Anything that has to do with the Navy is popular just at present. We had got a Congressman to introduce and father an appropriation bill, and we could count upon the support of enough members of both houses to put it through. We wanted Congress to appropriate twenty thousand dollars. We hoped to raise another ten thousand dollars by popular subscription. Mr. Garlock could assure us two thousand dollars; Tremlidge would contribute twenty thousand dollars in the name of the Times, and I pledged myself to ten thousand dollars, and promised to build the ship's engines and fittings. We kept our intentions to ourselves, as Tremlidge did not want the other papers to get hold of the story before the Times printed it. But we continued to lay our wires at Washington. Everything was going as smooth as oil; we seemed sure of the success of our appropriation bill, and it was even to be introduced next week, when the news came of the collapse of the English expedition—the Duane-Parsons affair.

"You would have expected precisely an opposite effect, but it has knocked our chances with Congress into a cocked hat. Our member, who was to father the bill, declared to us that so sure as it was brought up now it would be killed in committee. I went to Washington at once; it was this, and not,

as you supposed, private business that has taken
me away. I saw our member and Tremlidge's head
correspondent. It was absolutely no use. These
men who have their finger upon the Congressional
pulse were all of the same opinion. It would be
useless to try to put through our bill at present.
Our member said ' Wait ; ' all Tremlidge's men said
' Wait—wait for another year, until this English
expedition and its failure are forgotten, and then
try again.' But we don't want to wait. Suppose
Duane *is* blocked for the present. He has a tremendous start. He's on the ground. By next summer
the chances are the ice will have so broken up as to
permit him to push ahead, and by the time our bill
gets through and our ship built and launched he
may be—heaven knows where, right up to the Pole,
perhaps. No, we can't afford to give England such
long odds. We want to lay the keel of our ship
as soon as we can—next week, if possible ; we've got
the balance of the summer and all the winter to prepare in, and a year from this month we want our
American expedition to be inside the polar circle,
to be up with Duane, and at least to break even with
England. If we can do that we're not afraid of the
result, provided," continued Mr. Campbell, " provided *you*, Mr. Bennett, are in command. If you
consent to make the attempt, only one point remains
to be settled. Congress has failed us. We will
give up the idea of an appropriation. Now, then,
and this is particularly what we want to consult
you about, how are we going to raise the twenty
thousand dollars ? "

Lloyd rose to her feet.

" You may draw on me for the amount," she said quietly.

Garlock uncrossed his legs and sat up abruptly in the deep-seated chair. Tremlidge screwed his monocle into his eye and stared, while Campbell turned about sharply at the sound of Lloyd's voice with a murmur of astonishment. Bennett alone did not move. As before, he leaned heavily against the mantelpiece, his hands in his pockets, his head and his huge shoulders a little bent. Only from under his thick, knotted frown he shot a swift glance toward his wife. Lloyd paid no attention to the others. After that one quiet movement that had brought her to her feet she remained motionless and erect, her hands hanging straight at her sides, the colour slowly mounting to her cheeks. She met Bennett's glance and held it steadily, calmly, looking straight into his eyes. She said no word, but all her love for him, all her hopes of him, all the fine, strong resolve that, come what would, his career should not be broken, his ambition should not faint through any weakness of hers, all her eager sympathy for his great work, all her strong, womanly encouragement for him to accomplish his destiny spoke to him, and called to him in that long, earnest look of her dull-blue eyes. Now she was no longer weak ; now she could face the dreary consequences that, for her, must follow the rousing of his dormant energy ; now was no longer the time for indirect appeal ; the screen was down between them. More eloquent than any spoken words was the calm, steady gaze in which she held his own.

There was a long silence while husband and

wife stood looking deep into each other's eyes. And then, as a certain slow kindling took place in his look, Lloyd saw that at last Bennett *understood*.

After that the conference broke up rapidly. Campbell, as the head and spokesman of the committee, noted the long, significant glance that had passed between Bennett and Lloyd, and, perhaps, vaguely divined that he had touched upon a matter of a particularly delicate and intimate nature. Something was in the air, something was passing between husband and wife in which the outside world had no concern—something not meant for him to see. He brought the interview to an end as quickly as possible. He begged of Bennett to consider this talk as a mere preliminary—a breaking of the ground. He would give Bennett time to think it over. Speaking for himself and the others, he was deeply impressed with that generous offer to meet the unexpected deficiency, but it had been made upon the spur of the moment. No doubt Mr. Bennett and his wife would wish to talk it over between themselves, to consider the whole matter. The committee temporarily had its headquarters in his (Campbell's) offices. He left Bennett the address. He would await his decision and answer there.

When the conference ended Bennett accompanied the members of the committee downstairs and to the front door of the house. The three had, with thanks and excuses. declined all invitations to dine at Medford with Bennett and his wife. They could conveniently catch the next train back to the City;

A Man's Woman

Campbell and Tremlidge were in a hurry to return
to their respective businesses.

The front gate closed.   Bennett was left alone.
He shut the front door of the house, and for an
instant stood leaning against it, his small eyes
twinkling under his frown, his glance straying aim-
lessly about amid the familiar objects of the hallway and adjoining rooms.   He was thoughtful, per-
turbed, tugging slowly at the ends of his mustache.
Slowly he ascended the stairs, gaining the landing
on the second floor and going on toward the half-
open door of the " workroom " he had just quitted.
Lloyd was uppermost in his mind.   He wanted her,
his wife, and that at once.   He was conscious that
a great thing had suddenly transpired; that all the
calm and infinitely happy life of the last year was
ruthlessly broken up; but in his mind there was
nothing more definite, nothing stronger than the
thought of his wife and the desire for her companionship and advice.

He came into the " workroom," closing the door
behind him with his heel, his hands deep in his
pockets.   Lloyd was still there, standing opposite
him as he entered.   She hardly seemed to have
moved while he had been gone.   They did not immediately speak.   Once more their eyes met.   Then
at length:

" Well, Lloyd? "

" Well, my husband? "

Bennett was about to answer—what, he hardly
knew; but at that moment there was a diversion.

The old boat's flag, the tattered little square of
faded stars and bars that had been used to mark the

277

line of many a weary march, had been hanging, as
usual, over the blue-print plans of the Freja on the
wall opposite the window. Inadequately fixed in
its place, the jar of the closing door as Bennett shut
it behind him dislodged it, and it fell to the floor
close beside him.

He stooped and picked it up, and, holding it in his
hand, turned toward the spot whence it had fallen.
He cast a glance at the wall above the plans of the
Freja, about to replace it, willing for the instant to
defer the momentous words he felt must soon be
spoken, willing to put off the inevitable a few
seconds longer.

" I don't know," he muttered, looking from the
flag to the empty wall-spaces about the room; " I
don't know just where to put this. Do you——"

" Don't you know? " interrupted Lloyd suddenly,
her blue eyes all alight.

" No," said Bennett; " I——"

Lloyd caught the flag from his hands and, with
one great sweep of her arm, drove its steel-shod
shaft full into the centre of the great chart of the
polar region, into the innermost concentric circle
where the Pole was marked.

" Put that flag there! " she cried.

XI.

That particular day in the last week in April was sombre and somewhat chilly, but there was little wind. The water of the harbour lay smooth as a sheet of tightly stretched gray silk. Overhead the sea-fog drifted gradually landward, descending, as it drifted, till the outlines of the City grew blurred and indistinct, resolving to a dim, vast mass, rugged with high-shouldered office buildings and bulging, balloon-like domes, confused and mysterious under the cloak of the fog. In the nearer foreground, along the lines of the wharves and docks, a wilderness of masts and spars of a tone just darker than the gray of the mist stood away from the blur of the background with the distinctness and delicacy of frost-work.

But amid all this grayness of sky and water and fog one distinguished certain black and shifting masses. They outlined every wharf, they banked every dock, every quay. Every small and inconsequent jetty had its fringe of black. Even the roofs of the buildings along the water-front were crested with the same dull-coloured mass.

It was the People, the crowd, rank upon rank, close-packed, expectant, thronging there upon the City's edge, swelling in size with the lapse of every minute, vast, conglomerate, restless, and throwing off into the stillness of the quiet gray air a prolonged, indefinite murmur, a monotonous minor note.

The surface of the bay was dotted over with all manner of craft black with people. Rowboats, perilously overcrowded, were everywhere. Ferryboats and excursion steamers, chartered for that day, heeled over almost to the water's edge with the unsteady weight of their passengers. Tugboats passed up and down similarly crowded and displaying the flags of various journals and news organisations—the News, the Press, the Times, and the Associated Press. Private yachts, trim and very graceful and gleaming with brass and varnish, slipped by with scarcely a ripple to mark their progress, while full in the centre of the bay, gigantic, solid, formidable, her grim, silent guns thrusting their snouts from her turrets, a great, white battleship rode motionless to her anchor.

An hour passed; noon came. At long intervals a faint seaward breeze compressed the fog, and high, sad-coloured clouds and a fine and penetrating rain came drizzling down. The crowds along the wharves grew denser and blacker. The numbers of yachts, boats, and steamers increased; even the yards and masts of the merchant-ships were dotted over with watchers.

Then, at length, from far up the bay there came a faint, a barely perceptible, droning sound, the sound of distant shouting. Instantly the crowds were alert, and a quick, surging movement rippled from end to end of the throng along the water-front. Its subdued murmur rose in pitch upon the second. Like a flock of agitated gulls, the boats in the har-

bour stirred nimbly from place to place; a belated
newspaper tug tore by, headed for the upper bay,
smoking fiercely, the water boiling from her bows.
From the battleship came the tap of a drum. The
excursion steamers and chartered ferryboats moved
to points of vantage and took position, occasionally
feeling the water with their paddles.

The distant, droning sound drew gradually nearer,
swelling in volume, and by degrees splitting into
innumerable component parts. One began to distinguish the various notes that contributed to its
volume—a sharp, quick volley of inarticulate shouts
or a cadenced cheer or a hoarse salvo of steam
whistles. Bells began to ring in different quarters
of the City.

Then all at once the advancing wave of sound
swept down like the rush of a great storm. A roar
as of the unchained wind leaped upward from those
banked and crowding masses. It swelled louder
and louder, deafening, inarticulate. A vast bellow
of exultation split the gray, low-hanging heavens.
Erect plumes of steam shot upward from the ferry
and excursion boats, but the noise of their whistles
was lost and drowned in the reverberation of that
mighty and prolonged clamour. But suddenly the
indeterminate thunder was pierced and dominated
by a sharp and deep-toned report, and a jet of white
smoke shot out from the flanks of the battleship.
Her guns had spoken. Instantly and from another
quarter of her hull came another jet of white smoke,
stabbed through with its thin, yellow flash, and
another abrupt clap of thunder shook the windows
of the City.

The boats that all the morning had been moving toward the upper bay were returning. They came slowly, a veritable fleet, steaming down the bay, headed for the open sea, beyond the entrance of the harbour, each crowded and careening to the very gunwales, each whistling with might and main.

And in their midst—the storm-centre round which this tempest of acclamation surged, the object on which so many eyes were focussed, the hope of an entire nation—one ship.

She was small and seemingly pitifully inadequate for the great adventure on which she was bound; her lines were short and ungraceful. From her clumsy iron-shod bow to her high, round stern, from her bulging sides to the summit of her short, powerful masts there was scant beauty in her. She was broad, blunt, evidently slow in her movements, and in the smooth waters of the bay seemed out of her element. But, for all that, she imparted an impression of compactness, the compactness of things dwarfed and stunted. Vast, indeed, would be the force that would crush those bulging flanks, so cunningly built, moreover, that the ship must slip and rise to any too great lateral pressure. Far above her waist rose her smokestack. Overhead upon the mainmast was affixed the crow's nest. Whaleboats and cutters swung from her davits, while all her decks were cumbered with barrels, with crates, with boxes and strangely shaped bales and cases.

She drew nearer, continuing that slow, proud progress down the bay, honoured as no visiting sovereign had ever been. The great white man-of-war dressed ship as she passed, and the ensign at her fighting-top dipped and rose again. At once there was a movement aboard the little outbound ship; one of her crew ran aft and hauled sharply at the halyards, and then at her peak there was broken out not the brilliant tri-coloured banner, gay and brave and clean, but a little length of bunting, tattered and soiled, a faded breadth of stars and bars, a veritable battle-flag, eloquent of strenuous endeavour, of fighting without quarter, and of hardship borne without flinching and without complaining.

The ship with her crowding escorts held onward. By degrees the City was passed; the bay narrowed oceanwards little by little. The throng of people, the boom of cannon, and the noise of shouting dropped astern. One by one the boats of the escorting squadron halted, drew off, and, turning with a parting blast of their whistles, headed back to the City. Only the larger, heavier steamers and the seagoing tugs still kept on their way. On either shore of the bay the houses began to dwindle, giving place to open fields, brown and sear under the scudding sea-fog, for now a wind was building up from out the east, and the surface of the bay had begun to ruffle.

Half a mile farther on the slow, huge, groundswells began to come in; a lighthouse was passed. Full in view, on ahead, stretched the open, empty waste of ocean. Another steamer turned back, then another, then another, then the last of the newspaper tugs. The fleet, reduced now to half a dozen craft, ploughed on through and over the groundswells, the ship they were escorting leading the way, her ragged little ensign straining stiff in the ocean wind. At the entrance of the bay, where the enclosing shores drew together and trailed off to surf-beaten sand-spits, three more of the escort halted, and, unwilling to face the tumbling expanse of the ocean, bleak and gray, turned homeward. Then just beyond the bar two more of the remaining boats fell off and headed Cityward; a third immediately did likewise. The outbound ship was left with only one companion.

But that one, a sturdy little sea-going tug, held close, close to the flank of the departing vessel, keeping even pace with her and lying alongside as nearly as she dared, for the fog had begun to thicken, and distant objects were shut from sight by occasional drifting patches.

On board the tug there was but one passenger—a woman. She stood upon the forward deck, holding to a stanchion with one strong, white hand, the strands of her bronze-red hair whipping across her face, the salt spray damp upon her cheeks. She was dressed in a long, brown ulster, its cape flying from her shoulders as the wind lifted it. Small as was the outgoing ship, the tug was still smaller, and its single passenger had to raise her eyes above her to see the figure of a man upon the bridge of the ship, a tall, heavily built figure, buttoned from heel to chin in a greatcoat, who stood there gripping the rail of the bridge with one hand, and from time to time giving an order to his sailing-master, who stood in the centre of the bridge before the compass and electric indicator.

Between the man upon the bridge and the woman on the forward deck of the tug there was from time to time a little conversation. They called to one another above the throbbing of the engines and the wash of the sea alongside, and in the sound of their voices there was a note of attempted cheerfulness. Practically they were alone, with the exception of the sailing-master on the bridge. The crew of the ship were nowhere in sight. On the tug no one but the woman was to be seen. All around them stretched the fog-ridden sea.

Then at last, in answer to a question from the man on the bridge, the woman said:

" Yes—I think I had better."

An order was given. The tug's bell rang in her engine-room, and the engine slowed and stopped. For some time the tug continued her headway, ranging alongside the ship as before. Then she began to fall behind, at first slowly, then with increasing swiftness. The outbound ship continued on her way, and between the two the water widened and widened. But the fog was thick; in another moment the two would be shut out from each other's sight. The moment of separation was come.

Then Lloyd, standing alone on that heaving deck, drew herself up to her full height, her head a little back, her blue eyes all alight, a smile upon her lips. She spoke no word. She made no gesture, but stood there, the smile yet upon her lips, erect, firm, motionless; looking steadily, calmly, proudly into Bennett's eyes as his ship carried him farther and farther away.

Suddenly the fog shut down. The two vessels were shut from each other's sight.

As Bennett stood leaning upon the rail of the

bridge behind him, his hands deep in the pockets
of his greatcoat, his eyes fixed on the visible strip
of water just ahead of his ship's prow, the sailing-
master, Adler, approached and saluted.

"Beg pardon, sir," he said, "we're just clear of
the last buoy; what's our course now, sir?"

Bennett glanced at the chart that Adler held and
then at the compass affixed to the rail of the bridge
close at hand. Quietly he answered:

"Due north."